THEODORE ROETHKE

Essays on the Poetry

EDITED BY ARNOLD STEIN

UNIVERSITY OF WASHINGTON PRESS   SEATTLE & LONDON

c

237139

Am Sted.

Frontispiece photograph by Mary Randlett

Theodore Roethke: Essays on the Poetry

Acknowledgments

Quotations from Theodore Roethke's poetry are taken from the following editions:

Open House (New York: Alfred A. Knopf, 1941);

The Lost Son and Other Poems (Garden City, N.Y.: Doubleday and Company, 1948);

Praise to the End! (Garden City, N.Y.: Doubleday and Company, 1951);

The Waking: Poems, 1933, 1953 (Garden City, N.Y.: Doubleday and Company, 1953);

Words for the Wind (Garden City, N.Y.: Doubleday and Company, 1958);

"I Am!" Says the Lamb (Garden City, N.Y.: Doubleday and Company, 1961);

Sequence, Sometimes Metaphysical (Iowa City, Iowa: The Stone Wall Press, 1963);

The Far Field (Garden City, N.Y.: Doubleday and Company, 1964).

Contents

Introduction

THE DIRECT AIM OF THIS BOOK IS TO EXTEND AND create understanding of Theodore Roethke's work as a poet. The indirect aim is to honor his memory. All the poets and critics who have contributed to this volume share a general conviction that Roethke was a distinctive force in modern letters and that he wrote poems the world will not want to forget. But general conviction ends here, and each of the nine essays that follow represents the efforts of one gifted reader to explain his understanding of Roethke's achievement. No one was asked to praise, or to adopt a particular approach or emphasis. The variety and unity of the book have been allowed to find their own balance. Areas of agreement reinforce each other, and that is good—all the better when agreement comes from differences in insight, emphasis, and detail. As for the disagreements, they prepare the groundwork for future efforts to appreciate separate poems, lines, images, themes, separate aspects of Roethke's craft and meaning, his development through the body of his work, the shape of his poetic vision.

The most valuable disagreement concerns the nature of Roethke's originality as a poet. Stephen Spender, asking that poetry "should open up new frontiers of consciousness in language," understandably turns to *The Lost Son* and *Praise to the End!* For many critics the poems of that period reveal Roethke at the height of his powers. Few readers (and almost no poets) are likely to minimize the breakthrough Roethke made in the poems that begin with *The Lost Son.* The important question is this: did the commanding new voice discovered in those poems realize all at once the range of expression that most deserves our admiring response, or was that new voice, however arresting in what it said, still more significant as a stage that had to be passed through? The most energetic denial of Roethke's continuing growth is made by W. D. Snodgrass. On the other hand, Denis Donoghue and Roy Harvey Pearce have written extensive accounts of a poetic growth marked by increasing depth of awareness and power of expression.

The majority opinion of this book is that Roethke's poetry changes and develops. Admittedly, the kinds of order found in Roethke are not of the self-evident sort; to future readers they may be apparent on first acquaintance, but not to present readers. It has taken time to learn the delicate interrelationships of his language. A poet's language is never wholly given to him. His personal idiom of feeling, his rhythms, the subtle changes of inflection and meaning which develop as his growing family of metaphors and symbols intimately speak to each other—all of these must establish themselves in slow, precarious, individual ways. The richness and precision come as gift only to the reader, though he may have to work to be worthy. Roethke's language gained that mysterious coherence we can somehow take for granted in the best poets, whose poems, if we let them, interpret each other. What may at first seem private and opaque, a breathless plunge into wholly personal experience, can turn into something lucid, an insight grounded in the intensely particular but expressing what is open to us all.

Rereading the poems with the sad certainty that there will be no new, unexpected poems to prove one not only wrong about the future but inept about the past and present performances, at least encourages an increased firmness in critical observation. Roethke's earliest poems now come in for some fresh study; the questions asked them are acute and rewarding. Similarly, poems he chose not to reprint, and those he revised after printing, or rearranged in a sequence that kept growing—these have much to tell us about his own search, both conscious and groping, for direction. (When his notebooks come to be studied we may learn about the poems that came quickly and surely, and the ones he fumbled with, abandoned, or resurrected.) The love poems which, so little time ago, seemed extraordinarily new, unlike anything on the literary horizon, a personal movement in another direction not yet clear, have begun to fall into place. They were unpredictable and astonishing, but from the perspective of the last poems the surprises appear to be in the grain. Some of the most interesting pages in this book help show how Roethke learned, through certain poems, the way that he was going. When we look back with close attention, we discover how many of the apparent uncertainties, reversals, aimlessnesses are like the suspended movements of the painter's hand when it is arrested and studied by the camera —a "shaking" that keeps it "steady," an accelerated process of contemplation that issues finally in miraculous decisiveness.

When the writing did not come or did not come well, Roethke felt threatened in an absolute way that few writers, I imagine, have experienced. The threat was constant, the intermissions frequent but brief. Cultivating the edge of the abyss not only kept him out, not only gave significant shape to the gaiety and dread in which otherwise he might have been lost; the creative act seemed to be a force which held

the very person together. If Roethke had stopped writing
for as long as a year; or if he had stopped believing that his
latest poems, however stuttering or unfinished, were advancing toward a point he would be glad in time to recognize, the
poet might never have been able to begin again. He consid-
ered himself in some ways a "Perpetual beginner," and he
was, marvelously so; if the thought gave him personal pain
he nevertheless understood that the condition, however
humiliating, was one authentic source of his power. But his
beginnings were precariously dependent upon continuity. He
was, it is evident, a conscious master of technique; he
worked unsparingly and developed great skill, but he seldom
felt easy or fluent; he had no illusion that he could deploy
his talents for more than a little while without establishing
some deeper contact, in which he was not master but pupil.
I do not think he could have survived a long silence. And
the work of my colleagues in this book, marking the inter-
connections in Roethke's poetry, the movements forward
and back, strengthens my conviction that if at any crucial
stage he had not been able to find the channels that only in
retrospect seem clear, the writing would have ended like one
of those terrible journeys he lived through: ". . . flying like
a bat deep into a narrowing tunnel," or "out a long penin-
sula," or "Churning in a snowdrift / Until the headlights
darken."

When I say that the creative act held him together, I have
something definite in mind. He was an extraordinary person,
gifted in many ways. Let me mention only one, as example.
He was a passionate teacher, proud of his power to delight
and move. Students responded to him—with hard work, discipline, and love. It was an intimate affair, never an imper-
sonal transmission of knowledge or skill. In some other ac-
tivities, not related to teaching, he plainly liked the feeling
of power and not seldom would dabble in masterful reveries

—though he quickly felt out of his depth or lost touch with his own sense of relationship. Furthermore, he liked the feeling of authority and yearned to achieve it in his own writing. But he had no use at all for the kind of authority that can be imposed in the classroom. Roethke was too proud and too humble, in his own ways, to speak as a man who had done things, who had proved his possession of certain valuable forms of knowledge. He could never have adjusted to living off his capital. The kind of teacher he was depended on his continuing to be a poet.

I do not want to give the impression that the state I have been describing was in any way a moral one or the product of conscious decision. He could and did transform his life in poetry. But he lacked common talents for sustaining himself at a more ordinary level of living. One had the frequent sense that the whole range of wit, knowledge, imagination, and sensitivity hung in the balance; that if the poetry stopped the teacher would not know where to begin, and that the whole personality would lose its recognizable shape.

All writers learn from their own writing, and it no longer seems difficult to believe that a lyric poet may learn the deepest things about himself during the intensities of composition. If he is the right poet we recognize in the self he discovers both the variety and the oneness of human nature, both the isolation and the relatedness of the human condition. He breaks through our own complacency, reigns over our feelings, troubles us with his own suffering and rewards us with the precious knowledge he gains, which becomes ours as intimately as if we had won it for ourselves. Best of all, his experiences emerge in permanent expression, beautifully authoritative. His expression is a monument that we admire from the outside, where it is hard, cold, and exact. When we re-enter, it renews itself; we are surprised and satisfied, again and again.

What contemplation was to some philosophers, composition was to Roethke. But the philosopher and the mystic began by divesting themselves of merely human concerns in the effort to recover essential being at the source. Roethke had to piece himself together, plunging again and again into old experiences, confronting the human concerns, trying to make sense of them, to sort them out, never able to reject them as alien to himself but needing to assimilate them before he could transform them. He succeeded, less by purgation than by transformation. In the greatest moments of the late poems he achieves a kind of personal clarity that approaches, from a different direction, the contemplative ideal.

Not that we can collect from his work a very large anthology in praise of the mind. The most memorable expressions take the other side. "A mind too active is no mind at all." Or this, far too often quoted, as if it represented a fixed opposition: "Reason? That dreary shed, that hutch for grubby schoolboys! / The hedgewren's song says something else." I want to come back to the opposition stated here and make something more of it, but one has to begin by recognizing that such a contrast came easily to him, sometimes perhaps too easily. He was troubled by the difference between his capacity to think things through analytically and his power to feel his way, in poetry, through uncharted courses of thought. He might heave with baffled scorn when a professional philosopher pretending to be Socrates quizzed him about the intellectual content of his poems, and he did not cultivate the virtue of moderation when describing forms of intellect toward which he felt hostile. But he nevertheless had a touching respect for genuine learning, and he could display generous admiration for many kinds of intelligence he did not himself possess. The dry, the sterile, and the pretentious he hated most of all; he was quick to see through their plausible disguises, for he had acquired a gift of recog-

nition by practicing upon his own disguises, forcing them on
until he wore them out.

For the attacks of false humility take sudden turns for the worse.
Lacking the candor of dogs, I kiss the departing air;
I'm untrue to my own excesses.

("Praise to the End!")

The man writing the poetry acquired and begot an order
of intelligence not available to him in his everyday pursuits.
As a person he had to flounder and struggle, harder than
most of us and in constant peril of losing everything he had
gained. But the intelligence is there, permanently on record.
The fears and hostilities which he expressed toward the intellect he felt as personal truth. It was only by acknowledging them that he could work through the limitations they
imposed.

To consider one of many possible examples, in "Meditations of an Old Woman" the speaker knows "the cold flesh-
less kiss of contraries." As she approaches her final illumination she can cry, "I'm released from the dreary dance of
opposites." But a little earlier she has expressed her own
version of the conflict between "Reason" and the "hedgewren's song": "O to be delivered from the rational into the
realm of pure song." The desire is authentic but the
specification, being personal, needs to be qualified. She comes
down from that high pitch of her declarative rhetoric and
composes another resolution, this time not of opposites but
of alternatives that resemble each other and must be
differentiated, tactfully but firmly. For dreariness inheres
not only in opposites. Therefore, the condition of true deliv-
erance is described as being "Not drearily bewitched, / But
sweetly daft." As an expression of human modesty it goes
far and comes under the general justification soon to be expressed: "I take the liberties a short life permits." But that

range of human modesty is not enough. She will also say, "I seek my own meekness," and therefore what is inadequate in the expression of human desire must be admitted, even while the desire itself is reaffirmed:

> To try to become like God
> Is far from becoming God.
> O, but I seek and care!
>
> I rock in my own dark,
> Thinking, God has need of me.
> The dead love the unborn.
>   ("What Can I Tell My Bones?")

The release does not depend on opposites that can be squared off against each other by wit or by any personal urgency for ultimate answers. Human desire is authenticated by God. Mortal and immortal meet in love. Love seeks and is sought. The old woman is rocking and thinking; her answer comes quietly, like a revelation that has been waiting for the right moment to appear; that moment seems to have required many preceding moments, not all of them free of error and personal distortion. The language of the answer related to God is beautifully simple. George Herbert could have called the lines a true hymn, in which "the soul unto the lines accords." And Herbert too believed that God has bound Himself by the laws of love:

> So our clay hearts, ev'n when we crouch
> To sing thy praises, make them lesse divine.
>   Yet either this,
>   Or none, thy portion is.
>   ("Miserie")

But the old woman does not rest with the large answer involving God. She comes down to something yet simpler, to wholly personal ground, affirming once more the dignity of individual human desire. When she composes her final resolution—"I'm wet with another life. / Yea, I have gone and stayed"—it is out of unacknowledged opposites, death and life, the opposites that most dominate the human imagination. In what is not said, in her not needing to acknowledge them, we have the sure evidence of her final release from their grip. Donne would have recognized the concealed argument as "a demonstration to my soul, and demonstration is the powerfullest proof."

"A field for revelation." There is no imminent danger that we shall make too much of Roethke as a nature poet, anguished and inspired by growing things, a Marvellian mower and gardener at once, and more imaginatively obsessed by the unfolding seed of childhood than even a Vaughan or a Traherne. But he is also at times a Marvell who has to fight more desperately, without rules, to achieve his order. He is not an intellectual poet like Donne or Herbert, though he admired and learned all that he could from them. He is a resourceful modern inventor of that "coarse short-hand of the subliminal depths," and his own "terror and dismay" seldom rose to "a grave philosophical language." But we shall do well not to rest with opposites that he confronted because he meant to overcome them. "A house for wisdom; a field for revelation."

In the earlier poems wisdom is mostly what is left after exhaustion. When it speaks in its own voice it is elusive, shrewd but shy, proverbial, sparing of breath, more provocative than assertive:

> What grace I have is enough.
> The lost have their own pace.
> The stalks ask something else.
> What the grave says,
> The nest denies.
>   ("Unfold! Unfold!")

Gradually the breath-span grows longer, and statement assumes a more stable responsibility in the developing context:

The spirit knows the flesh it must consume.

I learn by going where I have to go.

The right thing happens to the happy man.

The body and the soul know how to play
In that dark world where gods have lost their way.

But perhaps it is best simply to quote these, one after another:

Father, I'm far from home,
And I have gone nowhere.

A man goes far to find out what he is.

He does nothing we should want to describe as the domestication of revelation, and he does not seek wisdom directly, in spite of the increased prominence of direct statement. Where he achieves wisdom it is in motion, in the serious internal play of evolving forms, in the form that his whole work makes. But he moves toward a personal clarity that owes less to the violence against himself, to the struggles in "the subliminal depths"; and he can draw upon mastered experience without needing to renew the full cycle of agitation. The greatest of the last poems speak out in a voice it has taken a whole lifetime to deserve. Power and authority are there, but only to make possible the presence of that authentic human dignity which never seems original and is always unique.

"Being, not doing, is my first joy," he wrote in "The Abyss." He conceived of poetry as a form of contemplative being. It is a conception easier to maintain on the heights than in the jungle of early drafts. No man suffered more from not doing or felt more deeply the threat of loss of being in the stammering hesitations of doing. Between crea-

tive surges he might play with some thoughts of set forms
and themes—mere poetic doing. He would have loved to
write the words for a smashing stage success, with or without music. A few times, when he seemed to be wavering too
long over direction and was dispirited, I suggested things.
He never took them up, and I knew that he was right. He
often tried new poems on me, expecting absolute candor
along with immediate and comprehensive insight, which
would naturally issue in admiration. Not seldom I was pre-
sented with these poems over the telephone, a sobering experience. His response to criticism varied widely: sometimes
he would acknowledge a fault at once; some things he would
defend mildly in the face of my insistence, and change nothing; what he defended most loudly was often the first to be
changed. Most of the time I think he was testing his inner
doubts, hoping that a poem was finished, prepared to be bel-
ligerent in its defense, but wanting most to settle his own
feelings.

In retrospect, the control he exerted over his poetic life
seems miraculous. That life evolved in its own ways, making
severe demands on him; demands which he had to recognize, when they were the right ones, like a single voice of
personal truth in a clamoring mob; demands that only great
resources, austere discipline, and a powerful will could have
possibly satisfied. For he was also beset by false starts, by
spurious imaginings, by complicated fusions of real-and-un-
real out of a commanding memory of the past which included the experiences of real madness. He waited, with surface fretfulness, anger, despair, but with enduring patience
and with a profound intuition of what was right and when.

In conclusion, I have some acknowledgments to make.
The original suggestion for the book came to me from Don-
ald R. Ellegood, Robert B. Heilman, and Glenn Leggett. As

editor I am indebted to them for advice and encouragement. I want to thank Beatrice Roethke for the helpful interest she has taken in the growth of this book. My final acknowledgment is not an editorial one and does not easily fit into established categories. It is good to be able to say that Theodore Roethke was given, in generous measure, the kind of support he needed as poet and as person—from students and colleagues at the University of Washington, from friends in the larger community. One does not take it for granted that in a publicly supported institution of higher learning, or anywhere else in our society, creative achievement in poetry will receive admiration, loyalty, gratitude. I want to make particular acknowledgment to the following men for official actions corroborated by personal conviction: to Solomon Katz, Glenn Leggett, Frederick P. Thieme, Charles E. Odegaard; and to Robert B. Heilman.

ARNOLD STEIN

May, 1965

Theodore Roethke: Essays on the Poetry

STEPHEN SPENDER

The Objective Ego

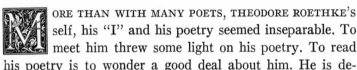ORE THAN WITH MANY POETS, THEODORE ROETHKE'S
self, his "I" and his poetry seemed inseparable. To
meet him threw some light on his poetry. To read
his poetry is to wonder a good deal about him. He is de-
cidedly not among the poets whose work fulfills T. S. Eliot's
injunction that poetry should be an "escape from personality." Not, though, that at his best, it is the "expression of
personality" either. The position of Roethke, which forms
so much a subject of his poems, is that he is to himself in-
escapable. To see things separate from himself is an aim
rarely achieved: "I could watch! I could watch! / I saw
the separateness of all things!" "Separateness" like "swaying" is a word that bears much weight of meaning in his
poems. It is not the separateness of things from one another which concerns him so deeply, but to see their separateness from himself. The development of his work is
from the child's absorption in the physical nature around
him, to confrontation with the polarity of people and things
outside—women, the woman!—and at the end the separation of spirit from body, the confrontation of death. This
development takes place before us like a very slow and
rather awkward dance ("dance" being another of his pivotal

words) expressed with much art. But through the art one sees the figure of the poet portrayed with almost primitive awkwardness like the poet and his muse in the painting of that name by Théodore Rousseau.

It is not frivolous to recall my impression on first meeting Theodore Roethke. This was in the early 1950's when I gave a reading at the University of Washington. I remember little of the reading except my being introduced by a man who was in every way of enormous size, "the poet in residence" whose name and work I did not then know. Introductory speeches vary, from the flattering ones which make the subject of them want to sink under the earth, to perfunctory recitals of the names of his works and achievements gleaned from some work of reference. It is rare for the introducer to get up and rebuke the speaker. But when my ears, taking over from my eyes fascinated by the gyrations like those of a weather vane slowly turning in the force of some gale unfelt by the rest of us—the swaying elephantine dance of his huge body—when my ears began to disentangle the words the poet in residence was saying—in sentences he seemed to unwind from his turning form like flax from a spindle—I found myself listening to a dirge, a complaint partly directed to me, but also partly a petition in his own favor directed at the audience.

Mr. Spender, he seemed to be saying, was one of these English poets, who come over to America—are received everywhere, paid, listened to, perhaps applauded. What made the speaker so sore was not that he knew himself to be a better poet than the one now about to read his poems to a credulous audience—but that Mr. Spender was going to be paid more than the introducer received on the occasions when he gave a reading.

There was, though, self-mockery in his mockery, a courtesy of including me in his act. Afterwards he said or wrote to me that it was all love-hate—if he didn't love me he would never have said those hard things. Love-hate provided, I suspect, his norm in his relationship with others.

Many years later, on another occasion, I happened to observe Roethke when he was reading his own poems. He was introduced by the chairman of the English department at a midwestern university, who was, perhaps, a bit overelaborate (through nervousness I suspect) in his introduction. After a few minutes of hearing his virtues analyzed, Roethke, who was strategically seated well behind the chairman, spread out his arms in an enormous shrug, twisted his head, fidgeted in his chair, heaved enormous sighs, and pulled lamentable faces. It was a gigantic act of dissociation from what was being said about him. I do not know whether the chairman knew what was going on. Being a well-disposed and very modest man, if he had done so I think he would have found little cause for offense in Roethke's apparent offensiveness, which was somehow so much his own private affair (however publicly he displayed it), as to be no concern of the chairman. We, the audience, were witnessing Roethke's separateness in his own self-involvement.

In his poems, Roethke seems often to be dancing. This is not the dance transcended and purified in the poetry, the entry into a metaphysical pattern of theological joy of Auden or Eliot, nor is it the tragic dancing on the graves of the dead of Yeats—it is simply Roethke incredibly and almost against his will dancing. He is the boy who is waltzed round by his father of the whiskeyed breath; the sensual man swaying toward the woman swaying toward him; the dying man dancing his way out of his body toward God.

There was never, one might say, such ungainly yet compulsive dancing, as in Roethke:

I tried to fling my shadow at the moon,
The while my blood leapt with a wordless song.
Though dancing needs a master, I had none
To teach my toes to listen to my tongue.
                              ("The Dance")

Roethke's poetry brings to my mind one of those measuring posts, standing in a stream, which records the depth
of the water. A line high up indicates where once a flood
reached. The lowest markings underwater are silted over
with mud, obliterated with green slime. Roethke's mind is
planted like such a measuring rod into his sensual life
through which there passes time, a stream sometimes flood-
ing, sometimes subsiding low, among the stone slabs, the
minnows, the weeds.

The measure of a grain of sand, and of nibblings of almost microscopic parasitic mouths is his authentic scale. It
provides a mean to which one relates the rest of his work.
One learns to bear with his rhetoric, but with no poet is one
more distrustful of what is called "development." Applying
the measure of the moment of the "I" which exactly en-
closes the object perceived, one is suspicious of a more ex-
pansive movement imposed by the poet's yearning after
effects of "greatness." "What sensual eye can keep an image
pure, / Leaning across a sill to greet the dawn?"

There is this Yeats-obsessed ambitious side of Roethke
(reflecting perhaps his body seemingly designed for gran-
diose gestures), one is impressed by this; but what one loves
is the poet of Beatrix Potter details, not the rhapsodic
bard. What is unique in him is an ambiguity itself ambiguous: a manner of escaping from a self which seems snail-like,
mouse-like, animal, vegetable, mineral, into an outsideness
which turns out to be the reflection of this miniature inner
world. There are transitions from inner to outer, self to not-

self, in lines which suggest some bright-eyed animal seen at
the entrance of its hole, peeping out, withdrawing again:

> Where do the roots go?
>> Look down under the leaves.
> Who put the moss there?
>> These stones have been here too long.
> Who stunned the dirt into noise?
>> Ask the mole, he knows.
> I feel the slime of a wet nest.
>> Beware Mother Mildew.
> Nibble again, fish nerves.
>>> ("The Pit")

and this goes on:

> At the wood's mouth,
> By the cave's door,
> I listened to something
> I had heard before.
>
> Dogs of the groin
> Barked and howled,
> The sun was against me,
> The moon would not have me.
>> ("The Gibber")

There are influences in Roethke, most evident in his earliest
and latest work, less evident in that of the middle period. I
write "influences" because that is the appropriate word of
the critical vocabulary. But rather I would describe them as
props, braces, stays, supports, worn externally and often
with a somewhat awkward self-consciousness. One is re-
minded, in the early work, of Emily Dickinson, Walt Whitman, Robert Frost, W. H. Auden, perhaps Edmund Blunden
(in "Vernal Sentiment," I suspect). And I seem to recognize
an echo of my own voice, in the breathless manner of "O young

men O comrades" and "my parents kept me from children
who were rough," in "O my sister remember the stars the
tears the trains." Later there is W. B. Yeats, embarrass-
ingly present in lines such as

> I turned and turned again,
> A cold God-furious man
> Writhing until the last
> Forms of his secret life
> Lay with the dross of death.
>   ("The Exorcism")

There are also moments of Dylan Thomas, and, in "The
Long Waters," surely the D. H. Lawrence of *Birds, Beasts
and Flowers*.

The poems most uniquely Roethke are those in *The Lost
Son and Other Poems* and *Praise to the End!* In these the
originality is very "far gone," so much so that, a little further, and the reader would lose contact with the poet. It is
difficult to think of poems which derive more completely
from the fusion of the poet's isolated sensibility with a very
solitary experience, going back to his childhood in the greenhouses and gardens of his father's "floral establishment."
Here one finds not so much an influence as an identity of
method with that of Rimbaud. Paradoxical as it may seem,
in *The Lost Son* and *Praise to the End!*, Roethke in his
concentration on his own experience, his complete identification of the "I" with the surrounding objects seems nearer
than any other poet but Rimbaud himself to what Rimbaud
called "objective poetry." These two volumes could certainly answer the description of a poetry "chargé de
l'humanité, des animaux même." He would agree with the
description of his task as that of one who "devra faire
sentir, palper, écouter ses inventions; si ce qu'il rapporte de
là-bas a forme, il donne forme; si c'est informe, il donne de
l'informe. . . ."

Entering into his world—indeed becoming it—his world "là-bas"—where words become loam, and roots and snails and slugs lying among bright chips of jangles from nursery rhymes and gashed childhood memories—Roethke is forever on the edge of Rimbaud's goal of the systematic *dérèglement de tous les sens*. One does not know whether to rejoice with the poems or sympathize with the poet: for the disintegration which bore strange and marvelous fruit in his poetry caused tragic breakdowns in his life.

The paradox of such "objective" poetry is that while concentrated in the "I" it is not egotistic. The "I" becomes the medium, the conveyor of the material of the not-I. Sometimes chameleon-like it assumes into its own being the colors of the objects upon which it is laid. In Roethke the not-I— the things outside him—seem to become him, or he to become them; yet, although outside, they come into being through the processes of his profound subjectivity. That is, they do so in those of his poems which excellently observe Rimbaud's principle of what is formed finding its form, what is formless, its formlessness. The form finds itself in:

> Small winds made
> A chilly noise;
> The softest cove
> Cried for sound.
>
> Reached for a grape
> And the leaves changed;
> A stone's shape
> Became a clam.
>   ("A Field of Light")

The formlessness is formlessness in:

> Hello, hello. My nerves knew you, dear boy.
> Have you come to unhinge my shadow?
> Last night I slept in the pits of a tongue.

> The silver fish ran in and out of my special bindings;
> I grew tired of the ritual of names and the assistant
>   keeper of the mollusks. . . .
>   ("The Shape of the Fire")

The distinction between the "I" which becomes, as in the lines quoted above, dissolved in the object, and the "I" which stays outside the object—the man of letters—is amply demonstrated in Roethke's own work. The merely literary kind of subjectivity, the poet's pose, is apparent enough in lines like this:

> In purest song one plays the constant fool
> As changes shimmer in the inner eye.
> I stare and stare into a deepening pool
> And tell myself my image cannot die.
> I love myself; that's my one constancy.
> Oh, to be something else, yet still to be!
>   ("Infirmity")

If this is moving, it is because one sympathizes with the poet, tragic in his concern with his own tragedy. But one's interest in the poet here is not as absorbing as when he employs language so that each word becomes a thing or microscopic part of a thing—when he himself, while remaining intensely himself, yet disappears into these things so much outside himself, which yet could only occur inside him.

When Roethke writes in the Yeatsian grand manner, he becomes the egotist who burdens the reader with his problems. He is the egotistic-sublime, no doubt, nobly confessional, wonderfully candid, and always sincerely self-absorbed, but the ego still remains that of the conscious poet, put in the insane asylum, experiencing marital difficulties, hating money and wanting to make a great deal of it, the man of letters in our time.

One guesses that there were two sorts of conflict in Roethke, which are recorded indirectly in his poetry. One, the struggle of the poet to follow his genius, which led him recessively back into his nature-absorbed childhood. The other, the struggle of the man to grow up and to use his imaginative powers to assist his will in the process. There is no reason why the struggle for maturity in life should not have been identical with that for maturity in art. But unfortunately this does not seem to have been so in his case. His genius was too far determined by intense child-hood visions for him to be able to transfer (for example) his interest in organic nature into an equal interest in other people. He was not a free enough intellect to dominate the Yeatsian mode. From the point of view of his psychological maturity, his attempts to transform himself into a more or less typical university poet of our time, are marked by regressions into the world of slime and dust and snails and mildew. His strength was what—as a man trying to live in our world—he regarded as his weakness, that he remained a perpetual beginner:

> Beginner,
> Perpetual beginner,
> The soul knows not what to believe,
> In its small folds, stirring sluggishly,
> In the least place of its life,
> A pulse beyond nothingness,
> A fearful ignorance.
>   ("What Can I Tell My Bones?")

One is moved by his struggle to achieve separateness, if only to bring some of his best poems to what seems a tri-umphant conclusion. But his victories, though often beauti-ful, contain a whisper of failure, of defeat in a combat necessary for the man, but which for the poetry's sake perhaps would have been better unattempted. The characteristic ending of "The Long Alley" is an escape from darkness, from the womb, from disintegration into light:

That was a close knock. See what the will wants.
The air could flesh a dead stick. Sweet Jesus, make me sweat.
Are the flowers here? The birds are.
Shall I call the flowers?

> Come littlest, come tenderest,
> Come whispering over the small waters,
> Reach me rose, sweet one, still moist in the loam,
> Come, come out of the shade, the cool ways,
> The long alleys of string and stem;
> Bend down, small breathers, creepers and winders;
> Lean from the tiers and benches,
> Cyclamen dripping and lilies.

Lovely as the invocation to the rose is, its appeal lacks the concentrated authenticity, the richness and strangeness, and freedom of:

> Stay close. Must I kill something else?
> Can feathers eat me? There's no clue in the silt.
> This wind gives me scales. Have mercy, gristle:
> It's my last waltz with an old itch.
>   ("The Long Alley")

Not that Roethke lacks legitimate successes in a more conventional modern poetry. "Big Wind," "My Papa's Waltz," "Child on Top of a Greenhouse," and "Frau Bauman, Frau Schmidt, and Frau Schwartze," are highly successful exercises in vigorous, economical, imagistic, ironic writing. If Roethke had written nothing else, these poems, outstanding in any anthology of contemporary verse, would have made his name. But apart from such bull's eyes, what one asks of modern poetry is that it should open up new frontiers of consciousness in language. Roethke does this in passages of a few poems, which are among the most solitary, most absorbed into a world of microscopically lived impressions, ever written, and which make him in certain passages a great poet.

LOUIS L. MARTZ

A Greenhouse Eden

All appeared New, and Strange at the first, inexpressibly rare, and
Delightfull, and Beautifull. . . .

Boys and Girles Tumbling in the Street, and Playing, were moving
Jewels. I knew not that they were Born or should Die. . . . Eternity
was Manifest in the Light of the Day, and som thing infinit Behind
evry thing appeared: which talked with my Expectation and moved
my Desire.

The first Light which shined in my Infancy in its Primitiv and Innocent Clarity was totaly ecclypsed: insomuch that I was fain to learn
all again.

(Thomas Traherne, *Centuries*)

 HAD BEEN READING TRAHERNE IN THE DAYTIME, FOR
another purpose, and reading Roethke at night,
thinking of this essay. Gradually, almost impercep-
tibly, the two writers seemed to be flowing together, especially in the sequence of meditative poems, growing out of Eliot's
Quartets, that opens Roethke's new, posthumous volume, *The
Far Field*. This "North American Sequence" begins, as
Traherne's meditations begin, with "The Longing"—for a
lost happiness:

How comprehensive that felicity! . . .
A body with the motion of a soul. . . .

The light cries out, and I am there to hear—
I'd be beyond; I'd be beyond the moon,
Bare as a bud, and naked as a worm.

I would with the fish, the blackening salmon, and the mad
lemmings,
The children dancing, the flowers widening.

There are of course the important differences: Traherne's images of light, childhood, and nature, his explorations of the memory, are based upon a firmly argued structure of Augustinian and Platonic thought; while Roethke's use of these images derives from the discoveries of modern psychology, and his method of exploration is based upon the cultivation of the irrational nuance, the fleeting association. Traherne's writings are rational, didactic, doctrinal; and indeed his poetry often suffers badly from an excess of abstraction; whereas Roethke's poetry evades the rational and tends to strip away abstractions. Yet a common origin of strength is there: the belief that in the depths of the self lies a core of power, a source of light, a redemptive memory—although, as Roethke says, in his poetry "The redeemer comes a dark way."

Thus, in the second poem of this new sequence, "Meditation at Oyster River," the mind moves backward from the present scene, as the speaker watches "the first tide-ripples, moving, almost without sound, toward me." In this quiet, even the gulls make no sound,

Their cat-mewing over,
Their child-whimpering.

At last one long undulant ripple,
Blue-black from where I am sitting,
Makes almost a wave over a barrier of small stones,
Slapping lightly against a sunken log.

I dabble my toes in the brackish foam sliding forward,
Then retire to a rock higher up on the cliff-side.
The wind slackens, light as a moth fanning a stone:
A twilight wind, light as a child's breath
Turning not a leaf, not a ripple.

The imagery of childhood prepares the way for the rippling flood of memory, "The tongues of water, creeping in, quietly."

I shift on my rock, and I think:
Of the first trembling of a Michigan brook in April,
Over a lip of stone, the tiny rivulet;
And that wrist-thick cascade tumbling from a cleft rock,
Its spray holding a double rain-bow in early morning,
Small enough to be taken in, embraced, by two arms,—

Or of the frozen river, its ice piled against a bridge, until a blast breaks the jam "And the whole river begins to move forward, its bridges shaking." So the poem ends, with morning recovered at evening, and the spirit freed for its inward explorations:

Now, in this waning of light,
I rock with the motion of morning; . . .
Water's my will, and my way,
And the spirit runs, intermittently,
In and out of the small waves,
Runs with the intrepid shorebirds—
How graceful the small before danger!

The third poem, "Journey to the Interior," moves through arid memories of the deserts and prairies of the American West and Midwest, toward the rich recovery of the fourth poem, "The Long Waters," where the speaker returns to the seaside imagery of "Oyster River" and sees

. . . in the advancing and retreating waters
The shape that came from my sleep, weeping:

> The eternal one, the child, the swaying vine branch,
> The numinous ring around the opening flower. . . .

The mind is on the verge of its deepest discovery, which now is accomplished in the long, intimate memories of childhood that cover more than forty lines of the title poem, "The Far Field," where the mind recovers completely its early sense of unity with natural things:

I suffered for birds, for young rabbits caught in the mower,
My grief was not excessive.
For to come upon warblers in early May
Was to forget time and death:
How they filled the oriole's elm, a twittering restless cloud, all
    one morning,
And I watched and watched till my eyes blurred from the bird
    shapes,—
Cape May, Blackburnian, Cerulean,—
Moving, elusive as fish, fearless,
Hanging, bunched like young fruit, bending the end branches. . . .

Such images—mingling child, bird, fish, and fruit—represent, as the speaker says at the close of this poem: "The pure serene of memory in one man,— / A ripple widening from a single stone. . . ."

The final poem, "The Rose," is perhaps related to Eliot's various rose-images; indeed the connotations seem inevitable, in view of the many, apparently deliberate, echoes of the *Quartets* that run throughout this sequence, beginning with the question at the end of "The Longing": "Old men should be explorers?" In many ways the whole "North American Sequence" might be said to represent a sustained tribute to Eliot's fertilizing example; the sequence has, at any rate, absorbed the meditative method of the *Quartets*, and, working within its own free texture of associations, it moves toward a moment of the rose where the present flower in its setting of "wind-warped madronas" evokes the roses in the childhood Eden:

And I think of roses, roses,
White and red, in the wide six-hundred-foot greenhouses,
And my father standing astride the cement benches,
Lifting me high over the four-foot stems, the Mrs. Russells, and his own elaborate hybrids,
And how those flowerheads seemed to flow toward me, to beckon me, only a child, out of myself.

One would hardly have expected this conclusion, knowing the Roethke of the early 1930's, with his efforts in the current "metaphysical" mode, his admiration for Donne and Marvell, for conceits such as

> Till at the last the master-Wave
> Upon the Rock his Mother drave;
> And there she split against the Stone,
> In a *Cesarian Section.*
> (Marvell, "The Unfortunate Lover")

—a passage that he read gleefully to his classes in 1932. Along with these enthusiasms went, of course, an admiration for Allen Tate and John Crowe Ransom, for the Elinor Wylie of *Angels and Earthly Creatures,* for the taut lyrics of Louise Bogan's *Body of This Death;* for the young Stanley Kunitz of *Intellectual Things;* for authors in the metaphysical mode now almost forgotten, such as Alan Porter, in *The Signature of Pain;* and indeed for all the sort of poetry represented in Genevieve Taggard's superb anthology of metaphysical verse, *Circumference,* which he greatly admired. The world of metaphor that Roethke then frequented may be illustrated by a query he used to quote from Louise Bogan. "I wonder," she asked, according to Roethke, "I wonder whether time moves from right to left, or from left to right?"

The early harvest of these admirations is found in his first volume, *Open House,* where the dominant mode is the tersely-phrased, strictly-metered lyric, in quatrains or couplets; and the chief aim is summed up in the words the publisher used in 1930 to describe the poems in Kunitz' *Intellectual Things:* ". . . these poems express ideas as hard and glittering as quartz." Such is the mode of Roethke's poem, "The Adamant":

> Thought does not crush to stone.
> The great sledge drops in vain.
> Truth never is undone;
> Its shafts remain.
>
> The teeth of knitted gears
> Turn slowly through the night,
> But the true substance bears
> The hammer's weight.
>
> Compression cannot break
> A center so congealed;
> The tool can chip no flake:
> The core lies sealed.

This is precisely the kind of poem that Miss Taggard was describing in 1929 in her lively preface to *Circumference:* "Ideas being for this temperament as real as grass blades or locomotives, the poet's imagination is always riding the two horses in the circus, Idea and Fact; they gallop neck and neck in his work, he has a genius for both the concrete word and the dazzling concept." "To give an idea no form but itself, to show it as organic by an inner music, as if the bones of a skeleton were singing in their own rhythm—that is the technical obsession of the metaphysical poet." Something of this sort is found in the promise of the title poem in *Open House:*

> I'm naked to the bone,
> With nakedness my shield,
> Myself is what I wear:
> I keep the spirit spare.

Yet along with these attractive poems in the current mode one finds the presence of another way: in the nature-poems that make up a third of this volume. These too are somewhat metaphysical, in Miss Taggard's terms, echoing Emily Dickinson, Léonie Adams, and the early Frost; but they have nevertheless a quality that we can now see reaching toward another dimension. The celebration of the naked bone, the spare spirit, and the sealed core is not the central mode of Roethke; it is indeed the very opposite of his true motion, which is to unseal, to let flow forth, to nourish into growth, after the manner prefigured in his early poem, "The Light Comes Brighter":

> And soon a branch, part of a hidden scene,
> The leafy mind, that long was tightly furled,
> Will turn its private substance into green,
> And young shoots spread upon our inner world.

One poem, above all, in *Open House,* suggests a way out of this metaphysical sealing: it is the poem aptly entitled "The Premonition," which Roethke did not choose to include in his later volumes of collected, or selected, verse.

> Walking this field I remember
> Days of another summer.
> Oh that was long ago! I kept
> Close to the heels of my father,
> Matching his stride with half-steps
> Until we came to a river.
> He dipped his hand in the shallow:
> Water ran over and under
> Hair on a narrow wrist bone:

His image kept following after,—
Flashed with the sun in the ripple.
But when he stood up, that face
Was lost in a maze of water.

One can guess why Roethke did not include the poem, for it
is quite unlike anything else in this early volume: the frank
reminiscence, the utter naturalness and simplicity of the
language, the subtle use of terminal assonance (especially of
the "er" sound), in place of formal rhyme; the shimmer of
implication in place of the hard conceit; the evocation of a
mystery instead of the sharp precision of idea. Roethke was
in fact embarrassed by the open display of feeling here; ten
or fifteen years ago, in discussing this poem, he said that he
winced in reading that cry, "Oh that was long ago!" The
exact word he used, I think, was "corny." But now this
seems the one poem of *Open House* that clearly points the
way home, to Roethke's truest manner, the cultivation of
the inner force of memory. It points to the greenhouse memories that form the still point of his deepest imaginative
existence, and it finds its fulfillment in Roethke's posthumous volume, in the poem entitled simply "Otto"—his father's name, the name of the greenhouse owner, protector
and procreator of greenness:

He was the youngest son of a strange brood,
A Prussian who learned early to be rude
To fools and frauds: He does not put on airs
Who lived above a potting shed for years.
I think of him, and I think of his men,
As close to him as any kith or kin.
Max Laurisch had the greenest thumb of all. . . .

A house for flowers! House upon house they built,
Whether for love or out of obscure guilt
For ancestors who loved a warlike show,

Or Frenchmen killed a hundred years ago,
And yet still violent men, whose stacked-up guns
Killed every cat that neared their pheasant runs; . . .

In my mind's eye I see those fields of glass,
As I looked out at them from the high house,
Riding beneath the moon, hid from the moon,
Then slowly breaking whiter in the dawn;
When George the watchman's lantern dropped from sight
The long pipes knocked: it was the end of night.
I'd stand upon my bed, a sleepless child
Watching the waking of my father's world.—
O world so far away! O my lost world!

In this final stanza, with its appropriate echo of Thomas'
"Fern Hill" (Roethke's echoes of contemporary poets are,
I think, nearly always deliberate and functional)—Roethke
overcomes his embarrassment at open exclamation: the cry
is the full recognition of his true center, bursting out of this
poem's Yeatsian mode, as earlier the cry of "The Premonition" had burst out of the metaphysical.

There is, Roethke's development shows, no necessary relation between the metaphysical style and the genre of meditative poetry: the two modes coexisted, happily, in the
early part of the seventeenth century, but in Vaughan and
Traherne we can see that coexistence fading; as with
Roethke, the metaphysical style in these two writers is over-
laid upon a hidden center. The metaphysical mode of "wit,"
the "strong lines," the firm intellectual control, which Yeats
recreated in his later poetry, and which Roethke imitated so
successfully in his Yeatsian period of the 1950's—this mode
of writing is not essential to meditative poetry, though it
may help to cultivate that kind of poetry in some eras and
in some poets. But there are other ways, and for Roethke
the best way was found in the poems of *The Lost Son,* a volume of great beauty, in its individual poems, in its ordering,

its development, even in the fine pastel-drawing by Charles
Seide that graces the jacket: a green stem or twig or shoot,
faintly suggesting a rivulet, emerges out of dark patches
into a green light, all symbolizing the implications of the
volume, as in the second poem, "Cuttings, *later*":

> I can hear, underground, that sucking and sobbing,
> In my veins, in my bones I feel it,—
> The small waters seeping upward,
> The tight grains parting at last.
> When sprouts break out,
> Slippery as fish,
> I quail, lean to beginnings, sheath-wet.

So the poems of the greenhouse sequence (Part I of the
volume) move from the darkness of underground, as in
"Root Cellar":

> Bulbs broke out of boxes hunting for chinks in the dark,
> Shoots dangled and drooped, . . .
> Nothing would give up life:
> Even the dirt kept breathing a small breath.

Then to the "Forcing House," where all the vines and
shoots and flowers "pulse with the knocking pipes." And
from here to the introduction of the small boy, working as
"Weed Puller"

> Under the concrete benches,
> Hacking at black hairy roots,— . . .
> With everything blooming above me,
> Lilies, pale-pink cyclamen, roses,
> Whole fields lovely and inviolate,—
> Me down in that fetor of weeds,
> Crawling on all fours,
> Alive, in a slippery grave.

The word "grave," at the close of this scene of primitive
vigor and struggle, reminds us that death is never very far

away in these scenes of growth; as in any vision of pastoral innocence, the strength of the life-giving imagery cannot be felt without the constant sense of struggle against some threatening, antagonistic force. Thus in that breathing "Root Cellar" the shoots have "long yellow evil necks, like tropical snakes," and in the following poem, "Orchids," we see how these exotic blooms "lean over the path, / Adder-mouthed,"

> Swaying close to the face
> Coming out, soft and deceptive, . . .
>
> And at night,
> The faint moon falling through whitewashed glass,
> The heat going down
> So their musky smell comes even stronger,
> Drifting down from their mossy cradles:
> So many devouring infants!
> Soft luminescent fingers,
> Lips neither dead nor alive,
> Loose ghostly mouths
> Breathing.

The beauty of growth, we see, is ambiguous: one can never escape the presence of some poisonous threat. After this evocation of danger it is appropriate that the next poem, "Moss-Gathering," should recognize the funerary function of the greenhouse and make plain the fact that a greenhouse is not nature itself, but nature sophisticated by art:

To loosen with all ten fingers held wide and limber
And lift up a patch, dark-green, the kind for lining cemetery baskets,
Thick and cushiony, like an old-fashioned doormat,
The crumbling small hollow sticks on the underside mixed with roots,
And wintergreen berries and leaves still stuck to the top,—
That was moss-gathering.

But something always went out of me when I dug loose those
    carpets
Of green, or plunged to my elbows in the spongy yellowish moss
    of the marshes:
And afterwards I always felt mean, jogging back over the logging
    road,
As if I had broken the natural order of things in that swampland;
Disturbed some rhythm, old and of vast importance,
By pulling off flesh from the living planet;
As if I had committed, against the whole scheme of life, a
    desecration.

Those loose and open rhythms, the closely-observed details
of natural growth, the frank confession, the sense of a dese-
cration—these things evoke the spirit of D. H. Lawrence, to
whose works Roethke was deeply devoted in the early
1930's—another sign that his metaphysical mode of that
time was superimposed upon a deeper allegiance.

The next poem, "Big Wind," as Kenneth Burke has
shown in his indispensable essay on Roethke's "Vegetal Radicalism," is one of the best in the volume, with its greenhouse sailing like a great ship in the storm:

> She hove into the teeth of it,
> The core and pith of that ugly storm,
> Ploughing with her stiff prow,
> Bucking into the wind-waves
> That broke over the whole of her,
> Flailing her sides with spray,
> Flinging long strings of wet across the roof-top,
> Finally veering, wearing themselves out, merely
> Whistling thinly under the wind-vents;
> She sailed into the calm morning,
> Carrying her full cargo of roses.

("*into* the calm morning" is the original reading: "into" has
become "until" in the 1958 printing of this poem, but the

latter is, I hope, only a misprint, for "sailing into" is essential to the poem's dynamic, triumphant close.) "Big Wind" throws a special emphasis upon the physical properties of the greenhouse, its "manure-machine," its "steam-plant," its "rusty boiler," its "cypress window-frames"; all these details serve, like the similar images of "Forcing House," to stress the element of deliberate art in the creation of these flowers, an art now stressed more clearly in the two following poems, "Old Florist" and "Transplanting," where we see first

> That hump of a man bunching chrysanthemums
> Or pinching-back asters, or planting azaleas,
> Tamping and stamping dirt into pots,—

and then find ourselves

> Watching hands transplanting,
> Turning and tamping,
> Lifting the young plants with two fingers,
> Sifting in a palm-full of fresh loam. . . .

Such art is necessary for the growth of the flower—and of the boy—the poet suggests, in his delicate associative way, by leading us from the conclusion of "Transplanting" directly into a picture of the "Child on Top of a Greenhouse":

> The young horns winding and unwinding,
> Creaking their thin spines,
> The underleaves, the smallest buds
> Breaking into nakedness,
> The blossoms extending
> Out into the sweet air,
> The whole flower extending outward,
> Stretching and reaching.

The wind billowing out the seat of my britches,
My feet crackling splinters of glass and dried putty,
The half-grown chrysanthemums staring up like accusers,
Up through the streaked glass, flashing with sunlight,
A few white clouds all rushing eastward,
A line of elms plunging and tossing like horses,
And everyone, everyone pointing up and shouting!

After this, "Flower Dump" provides a subtle, ironic qual-
ification of this victorious, exultant scene, when we read of
the "beds of bloom pitched on a pile,"

> Everything limp
> But one tulip on top,
> One swaggering head
> Over the dying, the newly dead.

But the sequence ends with the triumph of art in one of the
most intricate of all these greenhouse growths, "Carnations," evoking

> A crisp hyacinthine coolness,
> Like that clear autumnal weather of eternity,
> The windless perpetual morning above a September cloud.

The sequence is one of the permanent achievements of
modern poetry: its poems deserve to cling to future antholo-
gies like Marvell's "Garden" or Wordsworth's poem about
the daffodils. But in Roethke's collected verse, we should
note, there is an intrusion, the poem "Frau Bauman, Frau
Schmidt, and Frau Schwartze," which is interposed between
"Old Florist" and "Transplanting." The insertion first occurred in Roethke's volume *The Waking*, where the poem is
carefully starred in the table of contents as a "New poem,
not published in original sequence"—but this note has dis-
appeared in *Words for the Wind*, where we are now most
likely to read the sequence. "Frau Bauman" was first pub-

lished in 1952, about four years after the completion of the
other poems in this series, at a time when Roethke's Yeatsian period was first strongly manifested: "I take this cadence from a man named Yeats," Roethke says in the final
section of *The Waking*. This long period of Yeatsian imita-
tion no doubt performed an essential function for Roethke:
after the intimate self-discoveries of *The Lost Son*, some
sort of mask, like the earlier mask of the metaphysicals, was
apparently needed for Roethke's further development: to
escape from the incoherencies of the new poems that appeared in *Praise to the End!*, to include a larger measure of
intellectual content, and to achieve a broader symbolic dimension. How this influence worked we can see well in
"Frau Bauman":

> Gone the three ancient ladies
> Who creaked on the greenhouse ladders,
> Reaching up white strings
> To wind, to wind
> The sweet-pea tendrils, the smilax. . . .

The three workers are like Fates, winding the tendrils
around the white strings; this kind of allusion, along with
the formal inversion of the opening line, indicates a departure from the natural idiom and the localized greenhouse
imagery of the original sequence. That departure accords
with the distance that this new poem places between the
child and the adult, by an overt description of the sadness of
the adult state, and also by a careful literary echo of Yeats's
poem, "The Magi":

I remember how they picked me up, a spindly kid,
Pinching and poking my thin ribs
Till I lay in their laps, laughing,
Weak as a whiffet;

Now, when I'm alone and cold in my bed,
They still hover over me,
These ancient leathery crones,
With their bandannas stiffened with sweat,
And their thorn-bitten wrists,
And their snuff-laden breath blowing lightly over me in my first
　sleep.

The echo is well handled, with an effect of wry humor, and the whole poem is finely done, in its way; but it breaks the natural, intimate presence of those earlier poems, and it ought to be printed elsewhere in future editions of Roethke's poetry.

Indeed, the whole volume, *The Lost Son*, ought to be read in its first integrity, which Roethke began to alter in 1951, in *Praise to the End!*, where the four long poems that conclude *The Lost Son* appear as the first four in a sequence of seven poems (later enlarged to eight in *The Waking*). This longer sequence is preceded in *Praise to the End!* by a new and highly experimental sequence which evidently attempts to create a surrealist ground of the subconscious from which the other sequence can develop. The new effect is in itself interesting, although the new poems of *Praise to the End!* too often destroy themselves by violent experiments in a Tom o' Bedlam style. Moreover, it is a serious loss to have the final poems of *The Lost Son* separated from the greenhouse sequence, which they echo and complete.

In *The Lost Son*, after those poems of the greenhouse Eden (Kenneth Burke cites Roethke as speaking of "the greenhouse—my symbol for the whole of life, a womb, a heaven-on-earth") Roethke has placed two brief sections containing a dozen miscellaneous poems: miscellaneous in subject matter, but not in their arrangement. The second section opens with a childhood romp with a somewhat tipsy father, moves to the sixteen-year-old working in the pickle factory, then to the adult, slave to offices, and overwhelmed by

> . . .the inexorable sadness of pencils,
> Neat in their boxes, dolor of pad and paper-weight,
> All the misery of manilla folders and mucilage, . . .
>
> ("Dolor")

and from there to other poems of desolation, including the powerful presentation of mental breakdown in a perfect poem, "The Return":

> A cold key let me in
> That self-infected lair;
> And I lay down with my life,
> With the rags and rotting clothes,
> With a stump of scraggy fang
> Bared for a hunter's boot.

The third section narrates a gradual recovery, slowly built up from an apprehension of "that cold, granitic slime" and from a remarkable tribute to the tenacious life and healing power of the smallest creatures, in "The Minimal":

> Squirmers in bogs,
> And bacterial creepers
> Wriggling through wounds
> Like elvers in ponds,
> Their wan mouths kissing the warm sutures,
> Cleaning and caressing,
> Creeping and healing.

Lastly, the fourth section of *The Lost Son* is comprised of Roethke's first sequence of longer poems, "The Lost Son," "The Long Alley," "A Field of Light," and "The Shape of the Fire." Kenneth Burke has analyzed these poems in admirable detail; what I should like to add here is twofold.

First, an impression of the meditative method in these poems, foreshadowing the associative technique of the new "North American Sequence"; and secondly, a view of the ways in which these poems complete and unify the whole volume, *The Lost Son.*

These four poems all work in the same general way, especially the first, second, and fourth, which are composed in five parts, with the last two parts representing the movement of the mind out of chaos into the light. The third poem, however, is composed in only three parts, and offers within itself a retrospective view of the development of the entire sequence. The method of exploration followed in all these poems is basically the same as that found in "Meditation at Oyster River" and the other poems of that later sequence: it consists of arousing, first, a flurry of images, as in one of those old glass spheres where one used to shake up a storm of snowflakes, and then watch them settle down around a clear landscape; or as in that poem by Frost where the speaker, watching the waters in a well, sees, or thinks he sees, a flash of truth at the bottom. The method may be found at work within the purview of a whole sequence, or within a poem in the sequence, or within a section of a poem in the sequence. The third section of "The Rose," for example, opens with a whirling catalogue of "American sounds," in deliberate tribute to Whitman, including everything from the bobolink to the bulldozer, but after a dozen of these mixed images, the mind at last focuses upon a central sound:

> I return to the twittering of swallows above water,
> And that sound, that single sound,
> When the mind remembers all,
> And gently the light enters the sleeping soul, . . .

Thus in the final sequence of *The Lost Son,* each poem opens with a flight from ordinary "reality" into the irrational, the animal, the realm of the fish, the rat, the mouse, the cat, the eel, the otter, the mole; there are many implications of a return to the womb: "I feel the slime of a wet nest." These primitive images are given in a mode of flickering, sometimes ranting, incoherence, simulating the breakup of established modes of consciousness. Then, out of all this apparent disarray of being, there arises the strict, clear, calm imagery of that greenhouse Eden: warmth, power, growth, movement toward the light, as in the fourth section of the title poem:

> There was always a single light
> Swinging by the fire-pit,
> Where the fireman pulled out roses,
> The big roses, the big bloody clinkers.

> Once I stayed all night,
> The light in the morning came slowly over the white
> Snow.
> There were many kinds of cool
> Air.
> Then came steam.

> Pipe-knock

(Kenneth Burke, in his comment on this poem, cites Roethke as authority for the interpretation that the "knock" is both the steam in the pipes and the knock of the father's smoking-pipe as he approaches, bringing ordered life to the scene:)

> Scurry of warm over small plants.
> Ordnung! Ordnung!
> Papa is coming!

> > A fine haze moved off the leaves;
> > Frost melted on far panes;

> The rose, the chrysanthemum turned toward the light.
> Even the hushed forms, the bent yellowy weeds
> Moved in a slow up-sway.

In each of the succeeding poems this coming of light out of the primordial darkness is stronger, steadier, more inclusive, until it brings us finally to the man of full maturity and conscious power, controlling his fate as he controls the oars of his boat on the water. In the fourth section of "The Long Alley" (matching the fourth section of "The Lost Son") the greenhouse imagery emerges like a dream under water and becomes identified with a vital force within the human memory:

> Come, come out of the shade, the cool ways,
> The long alleys of string and stem;
> Bend down, small breathers, creepers and winders;
> Lean from the tiers and benches,
> Cyclamen dripping and lilies.
> What fish-ways you have, littlest flowers,
> Swaying over the walks, in the watery air,
> Drowsing in soft light, petals pulsing.

That word "drowsing" is important: it relates to the "watery drowse" of the next poem here, and to the "simple drowse" of the final poem; it looks back to the first line of the entire volume: "Sticks-in-a-drowse droop over sugary loam. . . ." It suggests a dream-like state of potential regeneration, where the stems of the mind renew their vitality, as in the climax of "The Long Alley":

> Light airs! Light airs! A pierce of angels!
> The leaves, the leaves become me!
> The tendrils have me!

In "A Field of Light" the growing mind moves toward a higher state of renewed consciousness, as it goes beyond the

greenhouse to apprehend the unique individuality of living
things:

> I touched the ground, the ground warmed by the killdeer,
> The salt laughed and the stones;
> The ferns had their ways, and the pulsing lizards,
> And the new plants, still awkward in their soil,
> The lovely diminutives.
>
> I could watch! I could watch!
> I saw the separateness of all things! . . .
> And I walked, I walked through the light air;
> I moved with the morning.

Finally, in the last two sections of "The Shape of the
Fire," childhood and maturity are placed side by side in
their proper dimensions, as the adult mind, knowing its
powers, judges the state of childhood, with all its easy beauty, inferior to its ultimate growth. The fourth section leans
backward toward the early state of the natural stem:

Morning-fair, follow me further back
Into that minnowy world of weeds and ditches. . . .

That air and shine: and the flicker's loud summer call:
The bearded boards in the stream and the all of apples;
The glad hen on the hill; and the trellis humming.
Death was not. I lived in a simple drowse:
Hands and hair moved through a dream of wakening blossoms.

But the final section presents the power of the full growth:

> To have the whole air!
> The light, the full sun
> Coming down on the flowerheads. . . .

And the volume ends with two powerful, summarizing images. First the image of a tranquil being, in a moment of
deep thought, oars poised upon a lake for further rowing;

and then the companion-image of the flower's destiny: the transient perfection of the flower, set at last in its ultimate vase:

To follow the drops sliding from a lifted oar,
Held up, while the rower breathes, and the small boat drifts
   quietly shoreward;
To know that light falls and fills, often without our knowing,
As an opaque vase fills to the brim from a quick pouring,
Fills and trembles at the edge yet does not flow over,
Still holding and feeding the stem of the contained flower.

Roethke never surpassed the achievement of *The Lost Son,* though many of his later poems are filled to the same brim. In these green images Roethke reached the center of his memory and found his wholly individual idiom. "The Far Field" recovered in his last volume is the same interior region reached in "A Field of Light."

WILLIAM MEREDITH

A Steady Storm
of Correspondences
Theodore Roethke's Long Journey
Out of the Self *

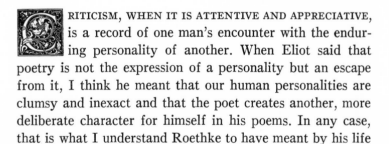RITICISM, WHEN IT IS ATTENTIVE AND APPRECIATIVE, is a record of one man's encounter with the enduring personality of another. When Eliot said that poetry is not the expression of a personality but an escape from it, I think he meant that our human personalities are clumsy and inexact and that the poet creates another, more deliberate character for himself in his poems. In any case, that is what I understand Roethke to have meant by his life work.

His published work, from *Open House* through *The Far Field,* creates one of those unmistakable human identities that make up the tradition of English poetry. They are of all sizes but, like the carp in an imperial pond, do not eat

* The title of this essay incorporates lines from two poems in *The Far Field:* "In a Dark Time" and "Journey to the Interior." The essay itself is a revision of a lecture originally delivered at Bennington College in 1963 in the Elizabeth Harrington Dickinson poetry lecture series.

one another, being sacred. Some are austere or eccentric and others we may simply not like. But all the writers who go on concerning us after their deaths are men and women who have escaped from a confused human identity into the identity they willed and consented to.

It seems sometimes to be casually assumed that it is harder to bring off an enduring artistic accomplishment today than in the past. This is probably one of our harmless provincialisms: the statistics suggest that it has always been next to impossible. In every time there are a few who shape their work—*instead of their lives,* it may seem—with a ruthless perfection. The intellect of man is forced to choose perfection of the life, or of the work, Yeats put it. Such work as the artist chooses is a door that must be unlocked deliberately, and I think of the boy in the fairy tale who cuts a key from the flesh of his own finger because he has no other substance. I can't feel that the twentieth century has been ingenious enough to make this job any harder. The poetry of Theodore Roethke is as remarkable for its deliberate movement toward a goal as for the success that attends it on its way.

The poems in *Open House,* his first book, not published until he was thirty-three, were marked by an elegance that was more than formal. The subjects were not tame—from the outset Roethke must have sensed that the genius inhabiting him was uncouth—but the issues of the poems were resolved by poetic formulas. The first of his recurrent poems about the discomfort of wearing flesh, for instance, concludes with these lines:

> Yet such is my unseemliness:
> I hate my epidermal dress,
> The savage blood's obscenity,
> The rags of my anatomy,

> And willingly would I dispense
> With false accouterments of sense,
> To sleep immodestly, a most
> Incarnadine and carnal ghost.
>   ("Epidermal Macabre")

It's a pretty conceit, verbally very pretty, but you feel that part of the emotion has been lopped off to make it come out like a proper metaphysical poem, that it is, in fact, an inaccurate statement from a man who will later say things like "The flesh can make the spirit visible" and

> I teach my eyes to hear, my ears to see
> How body from spirit slowly does unwind
> Until we are pure spirit at the end.
>   ("Infirmity")

—certainly a more complex and affectionate vision of the flesh.

It seems to have been the aesthetic premise of the first book that poetry is obliged to set experience in order. In the little poem called "The Bat," notice not only the smoothness of the metrics—smooth to the point of unfeeling—but also the orderly summary at the end.

> By day the bat is cousin to the mouse.
> He likes the attic of an aging house.
>
> His fingers make a hat about his head.
> His pulse beat is so slow we think him dead.
>
> He loops in crazy figures half the night
> Among the trees that face the corner light.
>
> But when he brushes up against a screen,
> We are afraid of what our eyes have seen:
>
> For something is amiss or out of place
> When mice with wings can wear a human face.

The suggestiveness of "We are afraid of what our eyes have seen," a line that throws the reader back on his own resources of fright, as good spookery does, is dispelled by the sheer tidiness of the last couplet that tells how and why to be afraid.

One of the most successful short lyrics in *Open House* is called "Mid-Country Blow." Here the experience itself is beautifully articulate and cleanly defined; it is not, therefore, diminished by the perfection of form and image with which it is realized. But what is striking about it, all these years later, is that it is not recognizably a Roethke poem at all. If someone told you it was by Robert Frost or Richard Wilbur, you might believe him—you could compare it with "Bereft" by one or with "Pity" by the other sooner than with one of the greenhouse poems.

> All night and all day the wind roared in the trees,
> Until I could think there were waves rolling high as
>   my bedroom floor;
> When I stood at the window, an elm bough swept to my knees;
> The blue spruce lashed like a surf at the door.
>
> The second dawn I would not have believed:
> The oak stood with each leaf stiff as a bell.
> When I looked at the altered scene, my eye was undeceived,
> But my ear still kept the sound of the sea like a shell.

Open House was, in fact, a stylish apprentice work. Like Frost's *A Boy's Will*, we return to it more because of what comes out of it than what was in it. We can admire a certain doggedness with which Roethke runs through his exercises in the genres of the forties. The poem called "Sale," for instance, which presents the decline of a great family in terms of an auction, is in the style of W. H. Auden's satires, the style that inspired a lot of Karl Shapiro's first book published a year later. The tag line of each stanza is set off by a

dash, to nudge us with the fashionable irony. The book is
full of order, but it is mostly the order of artifice.

The Lost Son and Other Poems was published seven years
later, in 1948. It projects unmistakably the character of an
original poet. Even of the three poems that Roethke re-
moved from the volume in subsequent collections, only one
could conceivably be by anybody else: a skillful but slightly
modish poem called "Double Feature," and this is no exercise but only a poem less sure in its persona than the others.
The middle stanza is not quite in character:

> I dawdle with groups near the rickety pop-corn stand;
> Dally at shop windows, still reluctant to go;
> I teeter, heels hooked on the curb, scrape a toe;
> Or send off a car with vague lifts of a hand.

If that is out of character it is because this is the book of
the greenhouse poems—"the book I continue to think of as
the great one," his friend Stanley Kunitz wrote the summer
Roethke died. The greenhouse poems—just to name them is
to conjure a fierce vegetable kingdom: "Cuttings," "Root
Cellar," "Carnations," and the greatest one, inserted here
later, "Frau Bauman, Frau Schmidt, and Frau Schwartze."
They are themselves examples of vegetable energy, they
spill over into Roethke's first free verse, every line of which
seems as certain of its shape as an opening leaf. Roethke is
one of the few poets whose internal rhyme and assonance is
worth thinking about. This poem seems to be the product of
an ear attentive to every sort of order that can be found in
exact speech.

> That hump of a man bunching chrysanthemums
> Or pinching-back asters, or planting azaleas,
> Tamping and stamping dirt into pots,—
> How he could flick and pick
> Rotten leaves or yellowy petals,

Or scoop out a weed close to flourishing roots,
Or make the dust buzz with a light spray,
Or drown a bug in one spit of tobacco juice,
Or fan life into wilted sweet-peas with his hat,
Or stand all night watering roses, his feet blue in rubber boots.

("Old Florist")

There is a bigger aesthetic premise at work in this book, the premise that is to lead Roethke through the restless course of his work. Instead of ordering experience, these poems attend on experience with the conviction that there is order in it. However imperfectly his eye might see it or his voice might articulate it—and he went on writing occasional shapeless lines and passages all his life—this *revealed* order was the only one Roethke served from this time on. It led him to write some formless and unsuccessful poems, but it led through them to one of the affirmative bodies of work of his generation, and one of the most perceptive.

Along with the new freedom of form in this book, perhaps underlying it, is a freedom of association, an openness to metaphorical suggestion, and the fearful possibility, entertained to the last moment, that an order inimical to man's spirit might be discovered, or no order at all. More and more of the statements praise a wise and attentive passiveness, the attitude that was to flower in one of his final poems in the refrain, "The right thing happens to the happy man."

The second of the two poems called "Cuttings" moves by this trust in association. (I might say first that I think it is one of a great many poems that can be damaged by overt sexual interpretation. Insofar as we are sexual beings—and happily that is quite far—things lurk in our minds. But insofar as a skillful artist speaks of experience other than the sexual, we must suppose that he intends to treat other experience, and pay attention to that.)

This urge, wrestle, resurrection of dry sticks,
Cut stems struggling to put down feet,
What saint strained so much,
Rose on such lopped limbs to a new life?

I can hear, underground, that sucking and sobbing,
In my veins, in my bones I feel it,—
The small waters seeping upward,
The tight grains parting at last.
When sprouts break out,
Slippery as fish,
I quail, lean to beginnings, sheath-wet.
                              ("Cuttings, *later*")

The acceptance of disturbing and disorderly associations, and of the formal risks appropriate to them, culminates in four long poems at the end of *The Lost Son*. These were to be, in fact, the beginnings of another book somewhat the way a long poem called "Burnt Norton" was to lead its author into a larger scheme. Three years later Roethke published *Praise to the End!* and placed the four poems where they are, if not less obscure, at least better sustained by other poems. But the title poem, "The Lost Son," appears first of these four in the earlier book.

It is not an easy poem, yet the obscurity is that of a lucid dream, where only the causes and connections, not the facts or events, are in doubt. The causes seem to be the death of parents, the speaker's recognition of his aloneness, sealed off in his link of the chain of human life, and the loss of childhood and its illusion of order. The fourth section is another greenhouse poem and comes to its climax as the child's eyes see the father, the greenhouse keeper, arriving as a figure of beautiful and terrible order:

Once I stayed all night.
The light in the morning came slowly over the white
Snow.

> There were many kinds of cool
> Air.
> Then came steam.
>
> Pipe-knock.
>
> Scurry of warm over small plants.
> Ordnung! Ordnung!
> Papa is coming!

Another of these four poems, "A Field of Light," stands
alone in a recent anthology and is in fact a self-contained
lyric poem of slightly more than average difficulty. It treats
a child's vision of the world, not always with a child's vocabulary, and is reminiscent of Dylan Thomas' "Fern Hill"
but without Thomas' preoccupation with time. A few lines
at the end convey its grace:

> Listen, love,
> The fat lark sang in the field;
> I touched the ground, the ground warmed by the killdeer,
> The salt laughed and the stones;
> The ferns had their ways, and the pulsing lizards,
> And the new plants, still awkward in their soil,
> The lovely diminutives.
>
> I could watch! I could watch!
> I saw the separateness of all things!
> My heart lifted up with the great grasses;
> The weeds believed me, and the nesting birds.
> There were clouds making a rout of shapes crossing a
>   windbreak of cedars,
> And a bee shaking drops from a rain-soaked honeysuckle.
> The worms were delighted as wrens.
> And I walked, I walked through the light air;
> I moved with the morning.

These poems are later placed in the vague narrative of
Praise to the End!, the hardest of Roethke's books to read

and very likely the hardest to write. I suppose it must also
finally be accounted the least successful, but it commands
admiration as a feat of exploration. At this point in
Roethke's life (and if I were to guess at autobiographical
events, I would guess that his recurrent mental illness—a
humiliating and terrifying thing, surely, to a man of his
imagination—acted in unison with his natural daring) he
performed an experiment as brave and pig-headed as *The
Waste Land*. He seems to have trusted his poetic voice to
speak for itself, to have given control of the poems to his
subconscious the way a ouija-board player gives his mind to
the never-mind. And this seems not to have been a desperate
move, the act of a man who had run dry in a certain vein,
but rather the urge of an explorer who is led on by an unfolding continent, who may die landless, like Daniel Boone,
but will have seen on the far side of the hills.

What Roethke does in *Praise to the End!* may be com-
pared, again, to what Robert Lowell did in his *Life Studies*,
which started in the prose piece—to my mind greatly inferior to the poems it begot—called "91 Revere Street." The
two poets explore and identify them*selves*, the self being the
intermediary of all experience, in a way that it is possible
for people of a certain wholeness to do without egotism. In
Roethke's case, what he found was a poetic myth as durable
as Yeats's, though humbler. His humbler poetic talent was to
live off the revelation of this book for the rest of its natural
life in much the way that Yeats's poetry can be said to have
lived off *A Vision*.

Praise to the End! is an anatomy of Roethke's imagery
and sensibility. In the course of recounting a spiritual auto-
biography he tells us what he feels about cats and dogs, hot
and cold, father and mother, trees, weeds, birds, stones, and
fish, and about his special image, the wind. He goes over and
over them until he gets them right. The instrument of en-

quiry is a primitive one, the feelings of childhood. At a later time, when he has returned from this exploration and resumed the use of symmetrical forms, he will write in a villanelle, "We think by feeling. What is there to know?" *Praise to the End!* completes the process of casting off artificial form in favor of the organic. The book is a continuous feeling out of the structure of existence in contempt, or near contempt, of reason. Toward the end of the book the speaker says:

> Reason? That dreary shed, that hutch for grubby schoolboys!
> The hedgewren's song says something else.
> I care for a cat's cry and the hugs, live as water.
> I've traced these words in sand with a vestigial tail;
> Now the gills are beginning to cry.
> Such a sweet noise: I can't sleep for it.
> Bless me and the maze I'm in!
> Hello, thingy spirit.
>
> ("I Cry, Love! Love!")

Knowledge is *felt;* and this last passage suggests that the senses by which we accumulate it are prehuman and that human speech is as instinctive as that of the other creatures. There are a couple of interesting consequences of this position in the poems, repeated patterns of syntax that imply that our speech is primarily involuntary, an animal cry. One of these is a series of soft invocations, sometimes the address of a vulnerable creature to implacable forces, more often a fraternal appeal to the mercy of little things. The following are in their order in the poems but occur at least a poem apart. They are all given urgency by assonance or consonance or alliteration.

> God, give me a near, I hear flowers.

> Whisper me over, / Why don't you, begonia,

> Hear me, soft ears and roundy stones!

Leaves, do you like me any?

Soothe me, great groans of underneath, . . .

There are a number of other askings like these, but two that
occur in "The Lost Son" are particularly explicit. The poem
opens with a section called "The Flight" which deals with
death:

> At Woodlawn I heard the dead cry:
> I was lulled by the slamming of iron. . . .
> I shook the softening chalk of my bones,
> Saying,
> Snail, snail, glister me forward,
> Bird, soft-sigh me home.
> Worm, be with me.
> This is my hard time.

The third section, "The Gibber," contains these three lines:

What a small song. What slow clouds. What dark water.
Hath the rain a father? All the caves are ice. Only the snow's here.
I'm cold. I'm cold all over. Rub me in father and mother.

These little prayers suggest the vulnerability of childhood
and also the serious, irrational voice in which we talk to ourselves. It seems to me that these poems convey the act of
talking to oneself as well as "The Love Song of J. Alfred
Prufrock" does.

The other pattern of syntax that is repeated fairly often
is a sort of parody of the folk saying, a two-part proposition
that sounds profound but frequently makes no rational sense
at all:

> A tongue without song
>   —Can still whistle in a jug.

> When you find the wind
>   —Look for the white fire

> Who reads in bed
>   —Fornicates on the stove

The second pair of lines above is followed by this: "What a whelm of proverbs, Mr. Pinch!" and just before another set he says, "Dazzle me, dizzy aphorist, / Fling me a precept." I think these passages are a self-challenge. The technique of *Praise to the End!* has been to set down side by side, and without rational connectives, short, stark declarations of fact and questions with apparently irrelevant answers. These mock-aphorisms, thrown in at intervals, have the effect of calling into question the whole project: can knowledge be *worded,* once it has been felt? They do this by reminding us of the mindlessness of most human speech:

> Time for the flat-headed man. I recognize that listener,
> Him with the platitudes and rubber doughnuts,
> Melting at the knees, a varicose horror.
> Hello, hello. My nerves knew you, dear boy.
>   ("The Shape of the Fire")

But whether I have solved these patterns correctly or not, they are phrasings to which he reverted, in intensity and perplexity, for the rest of his career. In *The Far Field* we find them both: "Leaves, leaves, lean forth and tell me what I am," he asks in "The Sequel," and in "The Longing," the turgid opening poem of the posthumous collection, he vexes himself:

> To this extent I'm a stalk.
>   —How free; how all alone.
> Out of these nothings
>   —All beginnings come.

Praise to the End! is a gazetteer of Roethke's country, naming the places where his feelings reside. Sometimes he is tree. In separate poems these lines appear:

> When I stand, I'm almost a tree.

> Believe me, knot of gristle, I bleed like a tree
> I dream of nothing but boards

> I've more veins than a tree.

> Is he a bird or a tree? Not everyone can tell.

Sometimes he is a dog:

> Call off the dog, my paws are gone.

> I can't laugh at a procession of dogs.

> Up over a viaduct I came, to the snakes and sticks
>   of another winter,
> A two-legged dog hunting a new horizon of howls.

> I've crawled from the mire, alert as a saint or a dog.

The poems return to chosen words by the circling motion of the bug on a ouija board trying to find what it means. "Is circularity such a shame?" he asks in one poem. The most frequently repeated theme is the wind. It is named at least once in every poem. Later the collected poems would be called *Words for the Wind,* as though that were the chief of the powers he would propitiate. The wind seems to mean to him another self, all the trouble and delight of the world's weather, a witch-like white goddess who is his muse in a wordless existence, man's merciful destiny—more than one would suppose a word could be charged with.

Praise to the End!, although its prosody is less formal than any of Roethke's other books, shows a considerable variety of formal effects. The most strictly controlled are a series of nonsense rhymes that catch the tone of a child's voice making up language:

> Mips and ma the mooly moo,
> The likes of him is biting who,
> A cow's a care and who's a coo?—
> What footie does is final.
> ("Praise to the End!")

This is not unlike what Joyce does on the first page of the *Portrait of the Artist as a Young Man:* "Once upon a time and a very good time it was there was a moocow coming down along the road and this moocow along the road met a nicens little boy named baby Tuckoo."

The freest effect is a passage in the final poem which is set as prose and begins:

And now are we to have that pelludious Jesus-shimmer over all things, the animal's candid gaze, a shade less than feathers, light's broken speech revived, a ghostly going of tame bears, a bright moon on gleaming skin, a thing you cannot say to whisper and equal a Wound?

The word "pelludious" I do not find in the dictionary, and the whole brief passage is, I think, a representation of the state of fear that arises in fear for one's own reason. It is the state that Joyce represents later in the *Portrait* during Stephen's religious crisis:

. . . Faces were there; eyes; they waited and watched.

—We knew perfectly well of course that although it was bound to come to light he would find considerable difficulty in endeavoring to try to induce himself to try to endeavor to ascertain the spiritual plenipotentiary and so we knew perfectly well of course. . . .

The difference between Joyce and Roethke in both these cases includes a broader humor in Roethke, humor that accompanies most of the terror in his poems and is driven off only by the tenderness.

Some years after *Praise to the End!,* Roethke wrote of his formal purposes: "I have tried to transmute and purify

my 'life,' the sense of being defiled by it, and, latterly, in
longer poems which try in their rhythms to catch the very
movement of the mind itself." He wrote these longer poems
at intervals for the rest of his career, knowing their risks. At
least two poems in *The Far Field*—"The Longing" and
"The Abyss"—seem to me seriously marred by the rhyth-
mic meander of the bemused mind. In "The Abyss," we
know for sure that Roethke knows his trouble:

> Be with me, Whitman, maker of catalogues:
> For the world invades me again,
> And once more the tongues begin babbling.
> And the terrible hunger for objects quails me. . . .
>
> Too much reality can be a dazzle, a surfeit;
> Too close immediacy an exhaustion. . . .

If in *Praise to the End!* and from time to time forever
after he flirted with the slow rhythm of chaos, it was part of
the deliberate identification we are concerned with. Immediately after this volume, the poems clear like a brook. The
natural world returns as though a warped mirror had been
made straight. We recognize the images but they have cast
off their grotesques and difficulties, and the rhythms, even of
the free verse, become more musical. The "Elegy for Jane"
comes from this period. The imagery moves from animal to
vegetable to elemental without confusion, conveying the
lovely vitality and changeableness of the dead girl. The
rhythms of the irregular unrhymed lines are a demonstration,
as so many of Roethke's free verse poems have been, of
Pound's remark: "I think there is a 'fluid' as well as a
'solid' content, that some poems may have form as a tree
has form, some as water poured into a vase." In the final
volume there are some great, scraggly trees but they accom-
modate one of the great natural forces, a man's feeling.

It was perhaps because Roethke felt he had won through
to a sure identity that in his later poems he made free to
borrow meters, cadences, tones from other poets, but chiefly
from Yeats. Once he seems to have been annoyed at some
sly critic who discovered what he thought he had made obvious, for he wrote a little essay called "How to Write Like
Somebody Else." In the course of it he says, "I suggest the
central problem remains: whether a poem has been created." He quotes T. S. Eliot (a poet I believe he never
liked): ". . . bad poets imitate; good poets steal," and adds,
"In other words, take what you will with authority and see
that you give it another, or even better life, in the new context."

I think it must be admitted that the influence of Yeats is
too strong for Roethke in several of the published poems.
There are lines and whole stanzas in which the rhetorical
identity of Yeats—which is no mean identity—is stronger
than the sensible identity, the identity of sensibility, of
Roethke. Yet it is hard to think of another instance where a
first-rate poet engaged so personally and in maturity a talent greater than his own. It is characteristic of Roethke. He
knew he had tremendous authority in the sense that he uses
the word in the essay, and it was characteristic that he
wanted to match it against his master.

He speaks too, in this essay, of a technical difference between his verse and Yeats's.

In the pentameter, I end-stop almost every line. . . . This is not
necessarily a virtue—indeed from many points of view it is a limita-
tion. But it is part of an effort, however clumsy, to bring the language back to bare, hard, even terrible statement. All this Yeats,
himself a bowerbird if there ever was one, would have understood,
and, possibly, approved.

Ordnung! Ordnung! Papa is coming!

It is always an interesting contest. In most of the Yeatsian poems Roethke's character—alternately tenderer, more
blustering, and more humorous than Yeats's—makes a new
thing of what he steals. But here is a stanza from a poem
called "The Pure Fury" where I think the influence is not
digested.

> The pure admire the pure, and live alone;
> I love a woman with an empty face.
> Parmenides put Nothingness in place;
> She tries to think, and it flies loose again.
> How slow the changes of a golden mean:
> Great Boehme rooted all in Yes and No;
> At times my darling squeaks in pure Plato.

Against this must be set a dozen perfect poems where something from Yeats has been transformed into a new thing: his
ancestor poem has become "Otto," his meditative poem becomes "In a Dark Time," his poet poem becomes "Heard in
a Violent Ward":

> In heaven, too,
> You'd be institutionalized.
> But that's all right,—
> If they let you eat and swear
> With the likes of Blake,
> And Christopher Smart,
> And that sweet man, John Clare.

The character that the work of Roethke presents seems to
me as finished and distinct as any of his generation, perhaps
matched only by Robert Lowell and John Berryman. What
he does with it is both simpler and more affirmative than the
work of those two men. Affirmations of any size are the
great challenge of the artist. It is easier to achieve an identity, to see a unique vision, through misgivings, grievances,

despair, on the one hand, or through utopias, sentimental optimisms, on the other. Only a very large and assured artist can retain his sense of self while deferring to created order. But created order, revealed order, is the source of the great visions of art. The artist looks at the world to affirm what is there, to affirm *he knows not what,* until his work is done. He risks this homelessness:

> I sing the wind around
> And hear myself return
> To nothingness, alone.
> The loneliest thing I know
> Is my own mind at play.
> ("His Foreboding")

And in the end it is because we see the man clearly that we are able to see with his eyes. The refrain of the earlier villanelle, "We learn by going where we have to go," yielded finally the refrain of the late one: "The right thing happens to the happy man." This is the man Theodore Roethke worked fifty-five years to perfect.

JOHN WAIN

The Monocle of My
Sea-Faced Uncle

"See," drummed the taut masks, "how the dead ascend:
In the groin's endless coil a man is tangled."
(Dylan Thomas)

HE BASIC CHOICE OF ANY ARTIST IS THE SELECTION
of his main subject matter, and however slow a de-
veloper he is, this choice is usually made quite early.
It is a question, fundamentally, of striking a balance between interior and exterior reality. Each of us is conscious
of a huge, unchangeable reality "out there," beyond the con-
fines of his own personality. Societies govern themselves;
institutions live on from generation to generation; languages
are evolved by the collaboration of thousands of speakers;
laws, customs, and prejudices gather themselves into hard
knots: thus humanity shapes the world and the world shapes
humanity. From the earliest infancy we are engaged in coming to terms with this exterior reality, which we may (if
we are strong-willed) hope to modify a little in this or that
direction, but cannot ever imagine ourselves being able to
change widely or deeply. *We* must adapt to *it;* we must

learn its ways, its languages, its procedures, its rules both written and unwritten. The process of modification begins so early, and is so radical and unceasing, that we can never be sure which of our actions are spontaneous and which are learnt and contrived. So soon, and so thoroughly, do we learn to adapt, to make concessions, to bargain with the immutable, to satisfy our appetites while seeming not to satisfy them.

And all the time, nevertheless, we are conscious of an inward reality—a life that goes on at a level unreachable by language or rationalization, consisting of the instinctual drives, the animal routines of self-preservation and self-gratification, and the mind's nightly wanderings in its interior forest of metaphor. This inner reality, as I have said, is not quite untouched by the outward reality that surrounds and conditions it. Elements in our behavior that appear instinctive are—we discover to our surprise, when confronted with the evidence from anthropology—actually as social, as "conditioned," as catching the 8:05 to work in the morning. Even so, we feel a genuine difference between the reality inside us and the reality outside us. We continue to talk, and sometimes to act, as if we had sold only a certain part of ourselves to buy social peace. As if the inner kingdom were really inviolable, ruling itself by its own laws.

The history of the arts, during the last hundred-odd years, could be written tersely, and not altogether inadequately, in terms of this dual reality. First came half a century in which the artist was primarily interested in the outer reality, and the extent to which the inner reality had to compromise with it. Then came the upheaval we associate with "modernity"; since when the artist has been primarily interested in the inner reality, and the extent to which the outer reality has had to compromise with it.

The first stretch saw the heyday of the realistic novel, the age which took Flaubert literally when he declared, "The two Muses of modern literature are History and Science." In the second stretch we have the symbolism, the surrealism, the preoccupation with myth and archetype, the breaking-up of the parquet surface of the novel into dream and solipsism. Marx is the creation of the first period, Freud the instigator of the second.

I spoke of "striking a balance," and a balance is a compromise. Most artists—even Baudelaire, even Hopkins, even Kafka or Max Ernst or Stravinsky—have compromised. However single-minded their zeal to explore one landscape, they have allowed glimpses of the other. Offhand, I can think of only two literary artists, of any stature, who have refused compromise. One occurs in each of these periods. In the first, Émile Zola. In the second, Theodore Roethke.

The key words there, of course, are "of any stature." Obviously there were hundreds of minor novelists who took over, unexamined, Zola's large "scientific" attitude. And equally obviously the 1920's swarmed with surrealist poets who burrowed into the interior landscape as unhesitatingly as so many rabbits. But Zola remains a considerable novelist, Roethke a considerable poet. Zola believed that a writer could study human beings by putting them in a tank, reproducing the features of their natural habitat, and sitting by with a notebook. Since there was no tank, he had to study the creatures without the benefit of laboratory conditions, so that the ideal conformity and predictability were never present, except in his notebook. Undaunted, he made the notebook more and more logical and schematic as the actual human creatures about him became less and less classifiable. He insisted that, given this social pressure and that physical propensity, this inherited tendency and that economic pattern, human beings would behave in an utterly predictable manner. And they do—in his novels. Similarly, Roethke

turned his back on the mass of customs and adaptations that
shape a man's inner life, and wrote about those things that
the mind apprehends only through the intuitions of the
body. Does the mind *ever* apprehend anything solely
through the intuitions of the body? Such awkward questions
troubled him as little as they troubled Zola. Both men addressed themselves to the task of making a picture of the
world through the lenses they had selected, with superb energy and superb confidence. Both succeeded because of the
intensity of their vision. They saw what they did see with
such piercing sight that we can deduce the outline of those
things they did not see.

Roethke is an evangelical writer. The ideas that inhabit
his work are ideas of salvation. Perhaps "What shall I do to
be saved?" is the question that underlies all art. Certainly it
is arguable that art is constantly engaged in the endeavor to
break down the isolation of the human being. It seeks always to bring us into a fruitful contact with *something*. Either the reality within or the reality without. In Roethke's
case the intensity of his lyric gift sprang directly from the
hunger that raged at its center—a hunger for salvation.
Given that the original condition of the human being is one
of confusion and loneliness, given that everyone, once the
unthinking energy of youth has worn itself away, is in more
or less the same sad, lost state—where is salvation to be
found? What is happiness, fulfillment, completeness?

In his answers to these questions Roethke frequently reminds us of Wordsworth, except that he is free of the temp-
tation to systemize his findings in quasi-philosophical language; and that physical passion, which is by no means
overlooked in Wordsworth's scheme of things, is nevertheless much more central in Roethke's. "Passion's enough to
give / Shape to a random joy," he says in "Words for the

Wind." The solitary ecstasies that shake the individual man
leave nothing behind them except questioning and bewilder-
ment. Those ecstasies that link him to the woman of his
choice are richer and leave a residue. Hence the recurrent
theme of losing one's loneliness in sexual love.

"Four for Sir John Davies" is very much to our purpose
here. Davies had written a poem on dancing, full of images
of harmony and participation. Roethke engages the same
themes in specifically sexual terms.

> Between such animal and human heat
> I find myself perplexed. What is desire?—
> The impulse to make someone else complete?

And again, "Did each become the other in that play?"
These are questions. Yet they are questions that expect the
answer "Yes." The whole sequence, for that matter, is strung
on a series of interrogatives—over a dozen of them in these
sixteen stanzas. But the question marks that sprinkle the
page cannot cancel out the confident assertiveness of the
rhythm, taken, as the poet says, from "a man called Yeats"
—the last major poet to ban all hesitations from his work.

Reciprocated love, joyous participation in the rhythms to
which all nature dances, physical fulfillment: these form one
of the main avenues by which the individual spirit reaches
its goal. There is a rich vein here. Just as the positive theme
of fulfillment releases joy, so the negative theme of
fulfillment's absence gives rise to some magnificent lyrics of
tragedy. The following short poem, for instance, which I
quote entire:

> I came to a great door,
> Its lintel overhung
> With burr, bramble, and thorn;
> And when it swung, I saw
> A meadow, lush and green.

And there a great beast played,
A sportive, aimless one,
A shred of bone its horn,
And colloped round with fern.
It looked at me; it stared.

Swaying, I took its gaze;
Faltered; rose up again;
Rose but to lurch and fall,
Hard, on the gritty sill,
I lay; I languished there.

When I raised myself once more,
The great round eyes had gone.
The long lush grass lay still;
And I wept there, alone.
                    ("The Beast")

Roethke's symbolism is never esoteric; here, the green meadow of fulfillment is reached by a heavy door about whose
threshold sharp and forbidding plants grow. The "great
beast" is large and powerful, but not malicious; its "great
round eyes" are those of innocence; it is "aimless and sportive," rather like the endless delighted games of the lovers
absorbed in their sensual happiness. Its horn is not danger-
ous, being merely a shred of bone, and round it a green and
growing thing, fern, is playfully arranged ("colloped"). The
door is open, but it nevertheless proves impossible for the
"I" of the poem to get through; he falls on the gritty sill and
loses his chance of the oneness with that powerful and innocent being in the "long lush grass." The poem ends, as it
must, in loneliness and weeping.

This attempt to explore the nature of "joy" is important
to Roethke, as it is to most poets, but surrounding these
peaks there is a more level terrain of normal experience.

Normal *inward* experience, that is. Though Roethke grew
up in a setting that must have been exceptionally rich in op-
portunities for social observation, he remained utterly consistent in his exclusive concern for the inward life. Occasionally the lighter poems offer us a brief glimpse of what he
might have done had he at any time turned his gaze on the
outward scene—one thinks particularly of "Frau Bauman,
Frau Schmidt, and Frau Schwartze" or "Old Florist." Or
that later poem "Otto" collected in *The Far Field*, that domestic landscape painted with the steady brush-strokes of a
loving nostalgia:

> In my mind's eye I see those fields of glass,
> As I looked out at them from the high house,
> Riding beneath the moon, hid from the moon,
> Then slowly breaking whiter in the dawn;
> When George the watchman's lantern dropped from sight
> The long pipes knocked: it was the end of night.
> I'd stand upon my bed, a sleepless child
> Watching the waking of my father's world.—
> O world so far away! O my lost world!

But mostly the poet is intent, as he has the right to be, on
his sterner concerns.

The basis of Roethke's intense moments of union with the
essence of created life, those moments when "everything
comes to One, / As we dance on, dance on, dance on," is his
unfaltering sense of his own place in the scheme of creation.
To say that he "reveres life" sounds like the stalest kind of
cliché; every artist, every fully alive man, does so. Yet the
starting-point of Roethke's work is certainly this intensely
felt impulse to merge, to identify himself, to participate in
the naked processes of life itself. And at this point, of
course, we find ourselves back at that famous greenhouse.

Roethke—it is the one biographical fact about him that
one cannot help knowing—grew up in and around an enor-

mous greenhouse, which was the center of the family busi-
ness; they were, I understand, florists on a large scale. The
greenhouse occupies the same place in Roethke's poetic evolution as the hills and dales of the Lake District do in
Wordsworth's. It was here that he received those early mes-
sages from the deeper reality that underlies and supports
the quotidian reality of existence. Though it is one of the
most familiar of his short poems, let us have on the page the
whole of "Cuttings, *later*":

> This urge, wrestle, resurrection of dry sticks,
> Cut stems struggling to put down feet,
> What saint strained so much,
> Rose on such lopped limbs to a new life?
>
> I can hear, underground, that sucking and sobbing,
> In my veins, in my bones I feel it,—
> The small waters seeping upward,
> The tight grains parting at last.
> When sprouts break out,
> Slippery as fish,
> I quail, lean to beginnings, sheath-wet.

This is the second poem in that sequence from *The Lost Son*
which builds up a large-scale, vivid, rejoicing picture of
those greenhouse days. It is a wonderful sequence: I would
say that it marked a point of Roethke's emergence, from a
gifted minor poet among gifted minor poets, into a poet of
the first importance with something absolutely individual to
communicate. From beginning to end, it is full of joy—a
fact that, by itself, would make it stand out as unusual in
1948. And such joy! Savage, brooding, tender, lyrical,
shouting: a joy welling up pure and irresistible from the
mere presence of life.

> ... what a congress of stinks!—
> Roots ripe as old bait,
> Pulpy stems, rank, silo-rich,

Leaf mold, manure, lime, piled against slippery planks.
Nothing would give up life:
Even the dirt kept breathing a small breath.

Poets have always brooded on nonhuman life and imaginatively identified with it, from the bees in Virgil's *Georgics,* via Lovelace's Grasshopper, through the full-blown Romantic treatment of Nightingale, Skylark, and Lesser Celandine. Roethke embraces and goes beyond all this. He is a "nature poet" whose nature includes the slug, the fungus, the beetle: in "The Minimal" he even celebrates the microbe, and very effectively at that.

This poetic brooding on forms of life remote from ours has traditionally been directed by a presiding appetite for analogy. "Even as" the flower or bird does such-and-such, the poet himself does so-and-so. The nightingale comforts the ailing Keats because it is a type of the immortality of art; individual nightingales die, but since they all repeat the same song through century after century, they belong to a world of art that is immune to decay and death. Roethke has none of this tendency to excogitate. His meditations are not analogical. The participation they celebrate is entirely immediate.

For the fullest, least inhibited, most joyful statement of this creaturely sense of life, one turns to the poems collected in *Praise to the End!* This collection, irradiated by a huge and spontaneous rejoicing, is the Paradiso of Roethke's work, and it occurs just about half-way through his writing life. I quote from the title poem:

I believe! I believe!—
In the sparrow, happy on gravel;
In the winter-wasp, pulsing its wings in the sunlight;
I have been somewhere else; I remember the sea-faced uncles.
I hear, clearly, the heart of another singing,
Lighter than bells,
Softer than water.

I use the word "Paradiso" with no intention of flattering Roethke by throwing in large literary terms. There are moments when his vision of creation is as broad and piercing as Dante's, though it is subjective by comparison with the cosmogony Dante could take over from Aquinas. In a fragmentary and surrealist way, Roethke really does set his individual in a universal background. "Fishing, I caught myself behind the ears," he says in "Unfold! Unfold!," that remarkable poem which builds image upon image of—but the colorless word is quite inadequate—"evolution."

> I was privy to oily fungus and the algae of standing waters;
> Honored, on my return, by the ancient fellowship of rotten stems.
> I was pure as a worm on a leaf; I cherished the mold's children.
> Beetles sweetened my breath.
> I slept like an insect.

The whole poem is luminous with humility and joy; it makes no claim to "understand," only to take part and to thank. It does not contain the word "God," and therefore I never expect to meet it in an anthology of religious verse, but it is more religious than most of the poems one *does* find there. Especially since it plots a real spiritual progress, from the disconcerted questioning of the opening lines to the quiet affirmation of the ending. At the beginning, the poet is bewildered by the strange journey he feels himself to have made "by snails and by leaps of frog." It is no use trying to put the process into reverse, and yet he has deep misgivings. "I can't crawl back through those veins, / I ache for another choice." By the time we reach the beautifully cadenced lines that end the poem, the questioner has won through to a close-grained, untroubled acceptance.

> A house for wisdom; a field for revelation.
> Speak to the stones, and the stars answer.
> At first the visible obscures:
> Go where light is.

This fat can't laugh.
Only my salt has a chance.
I'll seek my own meekness.
What grace I have is enough.
The lost have their own pace.
The stalks ask something else.
What the grave says,
The nest denies.

In their harsh thickets
The dead thrash.
They help.

The implications of this poetry are tremendous. A statement like "What the grave says, / The nest denies" is meant to be taken quite literally, and if we do take it literally we find ourselves in a universe of ever-renewed astonishment and richness—an "anguish of concreteness," as the poet calls it. These are the poems that establish and define Roethke's central concerns. The subject matter of *Praise to the End!* is, quite simply, those things that stir him into being a poet in the first place. I pause to drive the point home, because I think that any criticism of Roethke's work must radiate outward from this natural center; anyone coming freshly to his work would do well to read *Praise to the End!* first, and then take in the earlier volumes with their slow but measured progress toward this full realization of his personal themes, and then the later poems with their subtler harmonies and their poignant fight against an encroaching blankness. Certainly it is these central poems that seem to be directly described in the most memorable and generous praise Roethke's poetry received during his lifetime, such as that paragraph in James Dickey's review of *Words for the Wind:*

The best of Roethke's poems are very nearly as frightening and necessary as "darkness was upon the face of the deep," and as simple and awesome as "let there be light." It is this world of perpetual genesis, his own genesis, recurring, continually available if only the perceiver is up to it in mind and body, that Roethke has somehow got down in words. The few objects that define his personality—stones, flowers, sunlight, wind, women, darkness, animals, fish, insects, birds—tell his entire story, and the changes and similarities he finds among them are his poems. They are simple, tragic, profound, and unutterably joyful.

This, if we like to put it so, is the "random joy" that is given a shape by passion. And what the love poems add to these poems of life, fertility, and evolution—the small breath of the dirt, the comradely memory of the sea-faced uncles—is precisely that the passion they tell of provides a focus for all the emotions arising from the poet's contemplation of the world. "Words for the Wind" is entirely explicit about this:

> The breath of a long root,
> The shy perimeter
> Of the unfolding rose,
> The green, the altered leaf,
> The oyster's weeping foot,
> And the incipient star—
> Are part of what she is.
> She wakes the ends of life.

The same poem affirms that the long process of the evolution of consciousness is independent of time. Things shift, but they do not change. The sea-faced uncles are always beside us. "Whatever was, still is, / Says a song tied to a tree."

But if Roethke's poetry has a Paradiso, it also has an Inferno. (No Purgatorio, however. I find no trace of a region of suffering which purifies and strengthens.) This Inferno is described most memorably in "The Lost Son," a sequence also included in *Praise to the End!* The five parts of "The

Lost Son" take us from the first wandering astray, through
the terror of "The Pit" and "The Gibber," back to order,
harmony, and the known place. Which turns out, of course,
to be the greenhouse. Nothing in Roethke's work is finer
than the courage with which he brings the greenhouse, in all
its simple matter-of-factness, into this symbolic landscape.
After the surrealistic nightmare—

> Is this the storm's heart? The ground is unstilling itself.
> My veins are running nowhere. Do the bones cast out their fire?
> Is the seed leaving the old bed? These buds are live as birds.
> Where, where are the tears of the world?

—we pass, suddenly and with a beautiful sense of release
from pain, to the humble certainties which are also miraculous.

> The way to the boiler was dark,
> Dark all the way,
> Over slippery cinders
> Through the long greenhouse.
>
> The roses kept breathing in the dark.
> They had many mouths to breathe with.
> My knees made little winds underneath
> Where the weeds slept.
>
> > There was always a single light
> > Swinging by the fire-pit,
> > Where the fireman pulled out roses,
> > The big roses, the big bloody clinkers.
> >
> > Once I stayed all night.
> > The light in the morning came slowly over the white
> > Snow.
> > There were many kinds of cool
> > Air.
> > Then came steam.

> Pipe-knock.

> Scurry of warm over small plants.
> Ordnung! Ordnung!
> Papa is coming!

"The Lost Son," in keeping with the generally accepting and rejoicing tone of the poems of this period, ends with a positive resolution to receive the message of life.

> Was it light?
> Was it light within?
> Was it light within light?
> Stillness becoming alive,
> Yet still?

> A lively understandable spirit
> Once entertained you.
> It will come again.
> Be still.
> Wait.

All the poems I have so far mentioned are to be found in *Words for the Wind,* a retrospective collection that was published—in England, at any rate—in 1957. That volume ends with two remarkable sequences in which the poet projects his imagination into lives that are running down toward their end. The first sequence, "The Dying Man," is not among Roethke's finest work, though it contains many memorable lines; its dependence on Yeats is too mechanical. The second, "Meditations of an Old Woman," though in form it draws heavily on the Eliot of *Four Quartets,* is a much more original work. The poems are irradiated by a beautiful, tender, imaginative sympathy. One feels that the personality behind them really *is* feminine, really *does* feel life ebbing away. What is more to my immediate point is that here, too, we find the Roethkean Inferno. Less fever-

ishly, more slowly and sadly, the old woman faces the fag-
end of her life, "love's worst ugly day." Her problem is to
find some courage and some hope, and her starting-point is
that at least she is not whitewashing her situation with
clichés and vague reassurances.

> It is difficult to say all things are well,
> When the worst is about to arrive;
> It is fatal to woo yourself,
> However graceful the posture.

> Loved heart, what can I say?
> When I was a lark, I sang;
> When I was a worm, I devoured.

> The self says, I am;
> The heart says, I am less;
> The spirit says, you are nothing.

> Mist alters the rocks. What can I tell my bones?
> My desire's a wind trapped in a cave.
> The spirit declares itself to these rocks.
> I'm a small stone, loose in the shale.
> Love is my wound.

> The wide streams go their way,
> The pond lapses back into a glassy silence.
> The cause of God in me—has it gone?
> Do these bones live? Can I live with these bones?
> Mother, mother of us all, tell me where I am!
> O to be delivered from the rational into the realm of pure song,
> My face on fire, close to the points of a star,
> A learned nimble girl,
> Not drearily bewitched,
> But sweetly daft.

> To try to become like God
> Is far from becoming God.
> O, but I seek and care!

> I rock in my own dark,
> Thinking, God has need of me.
> The dead love the unborn.

After the familiar Roethkean pattern, the woman climbs slowly up the winding stair of acceptance and participation. By the end of the sequence she is declaring,

> I take the liberties a short life permits—
> I seek my own meekness;
> I recover my tenderness by long looking.
> By midnight I love everything alive.
> Who took the darkness from the air?
> I'm wet with another life.
> Yea, I have gone and stayed.

She is "wet with another life" in the same fashion as the "I" of "Cuttings, *later*," who quails, leans to beginnings, sheath-wet. If the Inferno is isolation and separateness, the Paradiso is union. We can all, after our own fashion, find our way to the meadow where the great beast plays.

I have said that *Praise to the End!* occupies a central place in Roethke's poetry. But what does this mean in terms of his development? Am I saying that the ground slopes gradually upward to this Andean range, and then falls away?

On the contrary, there is a stylistic development that goes steadily onward from the beginning of his career to the end. The early poems collected in *Open House* are not juvenilia; they are the carefully pondered work of a poet already mature. If the full statement of his central themes had to wait until *Praise to the End!* ten years later, the direction in which his gift was moving must have been evident to the attentive reader from the beginning. And once the major themes had been stated, the work was by no means over. The force and richness of their presentation depended on the variety and subtlety with which they could be rehandled, restated, re-examined, allowed to live and develop themselves in poem after poem.

In one obvious sense Roethke's "development" was a straight, hard fight all along the line. His major problem, in everything that concerned the actual techniques of his verse, was to find his own individual rhythms and cadences. Perhaps because of the spontaneous outflowing of his imagination into anything he contemplated, he was one of those poets who find it almost impossible not to reproduce the *sound* of verse by other poets that they have admired—admired, that is, deeply enough to make it part of their very being. Roethke gave himself utterly to the poems he loved, and in return they claimed him and exacted their tribute from his gift. He is always reminding us of other poets: of Yeats, when he writes a strong, dramatic ten-syllable line or a lyric with a refrain; of Eliot, in those poems with a more leisured, prose-like rhythm; of Blake, or sometimes of Emily Dickinson, when he is in homely and gnomic vein. And behind these individually identifiable poets lies the hinterland of folk-rhyme and nonsense-verse, which he loved and brooded on as he brooded on the buds and stems in the greenhouse—because they were life and because to dwell on them gave him comfort and joy. In his lecture "Some Remarks on Rhythm,"[1] Roethke gives loving analyses of such verses as

> Hinx, minx, the old witch winks!
> The fat begins to fry!
> There's nobody home but Jumping Joan,
> And father, and mother, and I

and

> Oh father dear, do ships at sea,
> Have legs way down below?

[1] *Poetry,* XCVII (October, 1960), 35-46.

> Of course they do, you goosey you,
> Or else how could they go?

In the same lecture he says, "We all know that poetry is shot through with appeals to the unconsciousness, to the fears and desires that go far back into our childhood, into the imagination of the race."

This takes us back to the process I described at the beginning of this essay: the process whereby the concern for inner reality took over from the concern for outer reality. If the individual human being cannot alter the hard outlines of the reality outside himself, then to some extent he must alter the reality inside himself—or mask it, at least—to avoid a perpetual conflict. It follows that only the child, and the young child at that, is a completely free human being, since he has not yet started—or, at worst, only just started —the process of modification and adaptation. So that the poetry loved by children, which works directly on the unmodified identity via the "unconscious," becomes the starting-point for the poetry that can liberate the enslaved adult. Liberate him, that is, into an awareness of the complex miracle of life which he shares with the sea-faced uncles, the drop of water on the leaf, and the dirt that keeps breathing a small breath.

This is the background of Roethke's work. And his emergence into the foreground of an individual utterance is habitually in the shadow of one or other of his grand masters. This disadvantage, which made Roethke so easy a target for the disapproval of reviewers (among whom, I wince to recollect, I was one) haunted his work almost to the end. But not quite to the end. His last, posthumous collection, *The Far Field*, brings in the harvest of those years of single-minded dedication to poetry. There are still echoes, but they are, so to speak, licensed by the overarching Roethkean idiom. The sound and texture of these poems are refined and strengthened by an imagination that has passed through the fires of discipline.

With regard to subject matter, *The Far Field* makes no conspicuous forward move. The themes of these last poems are the themes of all Roethke's work: the interplay of human with nonhuman life, the quest for a peace and joy that represents individual salvation. Once or twice there are hints of a redistribution of emphasis: the word "God," which is not often met with in the poems of the forties and fifties, occurs more frequently here, and is evidently not used lightly: there are hints of a movement toward religious belief. "The Abyss," for instance, a very moving poem which describes the dark downward journey into the pit of a mental breakdown, has a definitely religious tinge in the sections that describe the slow, wavering, but joyful ascent back to stability and freedom. In its fifth section, where the upward movement begins, we find the very explicit lines "I am most immoderately married: / The Lord God has taken my heaviness away." The first of these two lines states a familiar Roethkean theme: isolation is a punishment and a torment, union is a blessing ("I see and suffer myself / In another being, at last"). But the second line adds an element that would not, I think, have been found in the poems of ten or fifteen years earlier.

Another slight change of emphasis—one could never call it a "difference"—in this last volume is a deeper insistence that the desired state of personal salvation is a *stillness*. "The Abyss" ends with the line "Being, not doing, is my first joy." In "The Long Waters," from the "North American Sequence," which achieves such a superb blending of introspection with vivid evocation of American sights and sounds, the poet gets near to defining the "lively understandable spirit" whose presence he discerned in *Praise to the End!*:

I see in the advancing and retreating waters
The shape that came from my sleep, weeping:
The eternal one, the child, the swaying vine branch,
The numinous ring around the opening flower,
The friend that runs before me on the windy headlands,
Neither voice nor vision.

Beatitude, in the Roethkean scheme, consists of nothing so tangible as a message, nothing that can be "known" in the sense of being excogitated and handed on in abstract form. It means, rather, a sense of union with a *presence*. I use the word after a long hesitation, knowing that it will inevitably lead to association with Yeats's "Presences / That passion, piety or affection knows." Such association is bound to mislead, for the Yeatsian Presences are fixed and stable by comparison with Roethke's "shape that comes from sleep." By intense and sustained contemplation, such as we find in lovers, nuns, philosophers, and mothers, the human spirit can will itself into a relationship with the chosen Presence— that is the Yeatsian position. Life can be heightened, raised to the intensity of art, purged of the trivial and the accidental. And Yeats was deadly serious in this, for he had so raised his own life. Roethke means something else, something closer to what Wordsworth meant when he spoke, in *The Waggoners*, of

> . . . a shy spirit in my heart
> That comes and goes—will sometimes leap
> From hiding-places ten years deep.

These last poems of Roethke's are a summary, refined and strengthened by the power of his long-tried art, of what he had been perceiving and saying for twenty years. One short poem, which I quote in its entirety, could stand as a brief statement of his essential creed:

> Many arrivals make us live: the tree becoming
> Green, a bird tipping the topmost bough,
> A seed pushing itself beyond itself,
> The mole making its way through darkest ground,
> The worm, intrepid scholar of the soil—
> Do these analogies perplex? A sky with clouds,
> The motion of the moon, and waves at play,
> A sea-wind pausing in a summer tree.
>
> What does what it should do needs nothing more.
> The body moves, though slowly, toward desire.
> We come to something without knowing why.
>   ("The Manifestation")

But, of course, when we are dealing with poetry we are not dealing with "summaries," "brief statements," or "creeds." We are dealing with the way in which the poet, armed with whatever he chooses to carry in the way of beliefs and attitudes, goes out to meet the world. And in *The Far Field* Roethke's meeting with the world is richer and more delicate than anywhere previously except in the best passages of *Praise to the End!*

Since poetry is poetry and philosophy is philosophy, there is no such thing as a "philosophical poet." Nevertheless, it remains true that all poetry, all literature and art, is "philosophical" in the simple, etymological sense: it loves wisdom. And, having given an account, as sympathetically and sensitively as I can, of what Roethke's poetry does, it remains for me to indicate what I take to be its major limitations. It is too narrow in scope, too repetitious. It seeks for wisdom from one source and one source only. Of the various kinds of illumination a human life needs, this poetry pursues only one kind.

It would be easy to elaborate this statement in several

foolish ways. One can imagine, for instance, what a Soviet literary critic would make of Roethke's poetry.

Here is a poet [he would be obliged to say] widely successful, showered with prizes, employed to teach the art of poetry to students, fully acknowledged by the community—and his work contains no mention of the social realities of his day, no mention of the American people and their struggle toward liberty and prosperity, no mention of the bread-lines, the war, the racial upheavals, nothing about scientific progress, etc., etc.

And of course the whole laborious argument would be absurd. If "social realism" cannot produce a satisfactory account of the experience of Roethke's poetry—we should be justified in retorting—then "social realism" has provided one more example of its unfitness to offer an account of *any* literature.

But, in fact, the value of social-realist criticism is, often, that it forces us to define *why* it is inadequate, to say how its points might be made in a more sensitive and responsible way. What is wrong with Roethke's poetry is not that it doesn't mention the New Deal, Pearl Harbor, Little Rock, and socialized medicine, but that it doesn't enter the ordinary human world where these things have their effect. No, that in turn is an overstatement, a crude simplification. But we are getting nearer. The human world *is* there in these poems, but only in sharply limited areas. An old woman with her life running down, a child being weaned, a man making love to a woman or listening to the wind in the trees —these things are memorably and truthfully captured: and, beneath them, the basic subject of the human being as a creature. But there are other areas—of memory, of history, of personal relationships, of opinion, of custom—which we ordinarily inhabit, and which Roethke's poetry does not allow us, while we are under its sway, to revisit. When one thinks of the great poets whose accents are heard so insis-

tently in Roethke's work—when one thinks of Yeats, of
Eliot, of Blake—the difference leaps to the mind. They give
one a sense of total participation in life, he does not. Their
poetry meditates on inward things, and then walks out into
the air. His stays enclosed. His vision, intense as it is, remains monocular. Turn from Roethke to Pasternak, for example. In spite of the sparseness of Pasternak's poetry, its
economy and reticence, the range of human involvement is
total. Not in the sense in which Marxist criticism demands
this involvement, but in the true sense, that we respond to it
with our whole personalities. It takes up all the slack of our
minds.

I make this judgment reluctantly, because it is never
pleasant to point out the limitations of an artist who has
given one delight and left one's sensibility permanently the
richer, and Roethke has done these things for me. But without such a caveat, my analysis of his work would not ring
true. He is not, and we must say it plainly, one of those
poets in whose work we encounter the whole range of life.
Any fully alert mind, accustomed to participating in experience on all levels, will find that in the world of Roethke's
poetry, certain of its faculties become lulled, switched off.
And this, in the end, is claustrophobic and fatiguing. For
partial activity is constricting. Only total activity is lib-
erating.

I return, in conclusion, to a more positive note. Roethke's
poetry contains one element which, throughout most of this
essay, I have neglected. That element is thanksgiving. No
poet of our time, not even Dylan Thomas, has so aptly celebrated the divinity of life itself. One thinks especially of
Roethke's continual, spontaneous overflowings of thankful-
ness for the gift of light. So many of his poems, at their crucial moments, turn and give thanks for light. When this poet
says, "I hear the flowers drinking in their light," or "She

stayed in light, as leaves live in the wind," it is with a note of joyous authority derived from the scores of passages in his work which deal with this benediction of light. (It is worth recalling, in passing, that Roethke's poetry came strongly to my mind the first time I went into Coventry Cathedral, which is, of all buildings I have ever seen, the one organized most single-mindedly around this feeling of gratitude for light.) His poetry will retain its hold on our minds, by its strength, its ardor, its noble extravagances, its soaring passages of rhetoric which go on for pages without putting a foot to the ground; but most of all, perhaps, for the pure note of love and gratitude which it so consistently sounds. Let us give him voice at the end:

> To have the whole air!
> The light, the full sun
> Coming down on the flowerheads,
> The tendrils turning slowly,
> A slow snail-lifting, liquescent;
> To be by the rose
> Rising slowly out of its bed,
> Still as a child in its first loneliness;
> To see cyclamen veins become clearer in early sunlight,
> And mist lifting out of the brown cattails;
> To stare into the after-light, the glitter left on the lake's
>   surface,
> When the sun has fallen behind a wooded island;
> To follow the drops sliding from a lifted oar,
> Held up, while the rower breathes, and the small boat drifts
>   quietly shoreward;
> To know that light falls and fills, often without our knowing,
> As an opaque vase fills to the brim from a quick pouring,
> Fills and trembles at the edge yet does not flow over,
> Still holding and feeding the stem of the contained flower.
>   ("The Shape of the Fire")

W. D. SNODGRASS

"That Anguish
of Concreteness"—
Theodore Roethke's Career

HE CAREER OF THEODORE ROETHKE IS ONE OF THE most remarkable achievements of a period whose creative vigor will be a wonder to succeeding ages. Coming, as he did, at the end of that great revolution in the arts and sciences which began around 1850 and whose central aim was the dissolution of form and matter in every area (artistic, physical, intellectual, emotional, political, religious, domestic), he managed to sum up in his work this culture's war against form and even to advance that attack several steps further than anyone in his art had previously done. Yet coming after the destructive social revolutions which rose from the same emotional drives and accompanied the artistic and intellectual revolutions, it seems to me that he also summed up, in his ensuing flight from his own experimental drive, our peculiar inability to capitalize on our astounding achievements—our flight from freedom of form, our flight from the accesses of power which we have released. I must see this career, then, with an astonished awe, yet with sadness.

Roethke's struggle with form first revealed itself in his changing attitudes toward verse form and toward rhetorical and stylistic convention. This is typical: the general revolution against form and matter first found large-scale expression in the breaking down of artistic forms by the Impressionist painters and Symbolist poets. Seen from our vantage, Roethke's career is like a history of our artistic revolution in miniature.

Roethke's first book, *Open House,* seems surprisingly old-fashioned and prerevolutionary. The poems are open and easily graspable; the metric quite regular and conventional. There is even a romantic lyricism which verges on sentimentality and ladies' verse. Here is a typical example:

> O my sister remember the stars the tears the trains
> The woods in spring the leaves the scented lanes
> Recall the gradual dark the snow's unmeasured fall
> The naked fields the cloud's immaculate folds
> Recount each childhood pleasure: the skies of azure
> The pageantry of wings the eye's bright treasure.
>
> Keep faith with present joys refuse to choose
> Defer the vice of flesh the irrevocable choice
> Cherish the eyes the proud incredible poise
> Walk boldly my sister but do not deign to give
> Remain secure from pain preserve thy hate thy heart.
>
> ("To My Sister")

This was followed, however, by *The Lost Son and Other Poems*—almost entirely in free verse. A marked prosiness, too, came into the language texture, bringing very real success. Here appeared many favorite Roethke poems— "Frau Bauman, Frau Schmidt and Frau Schwartze," "Root Cellar," "Weed Puller," "Dolor," "The Minimal," and "Big Wind," which ends in a beautiful balance between lyricism and prosiness:

> . . . she rode it out,
> That old rose house,
> She hove into the teeth of it,
> The core and pith of that ugly storm,
> Ploughing with her stiff prow,
> Bucking into the wind-waves
> That broke over the whole of her,
> Flailing her sides with spray,
> Flinging long strings of wet across the roof-top,
> Finally veering, wearing themselves out, merely
> Whistling thinly under the wind-vents;
> She sailed until the calm morning,
> Carrying her full cargo of roses.

Also in that book, however, were poems which predicted the direction of Roethke's third book, *Praise to the End!*— a plunge into the wildest and most experimental poetry of the whole period. Though the poem quoted above is in free verse, we scarcely notice that. The verse flows easily and expressively, underlining the immediate meaning, drawing little attention to itself. It is nearly incredible that the same man could have written, in his next book:

> Believe me, knot of gristle, I bleed like a tree;
> I dream of nothing but boards;
> I could love a duck.
>
> Such music in a skin!
> A bird sings in the bush of your bones.
> Tufty, the water's loose.
> Bring me a finger. This dirt's lonesome for grass.
>   ("Give Way, Ye Gates")

Even after the wildest surrealists, that voice sounds new and astonishing; it could be no one but Roethke. It is an achieved style, carrying much meaning, and touching only tangentially other voices we have heard in poetry.

What's this? A dish for fat lips.
Who says? A nameless stranger.
Is he a bird or a tree? Not everyone can tell.

Water recedes to the crying of spiders.
An old scow bumps over black rocks.
A cracked pod calls.

Mother me out of here. What more will the bones allow?
Will the sea give the wind suck? A toad folds into a stone.
These flowers are all fangs. Comfort me, fury.
Wake me, witch, we'll do the dance of rotten sticks.

("The Shape of the Fire")

Even now, more than twelve years since those poems appeared, I do not feel that I really understand them, or feel certain how ultimately successful they are.

Yet that is not the point. The point, I think, is that Roethke had opened out before himself an incredible landscape. He had regressed into areas of the psyche where the powerful thoughts and feelings of the child—the raw materials and driving power of our later lives—remain under the layers of rationale and of civilized purpose. The explorations made possible by this book alone could have engaged a lifetime. Yet Roethke never seriously entered the area again.

It is not surprising that Roethke might at this point need to step back and regather his forces. He did just that in the group of "New Poems" which first appeared in *The Waking* and which were later called "Shorter Poems, 1951-53" in *Words for the Wind*. Here Roethke returned to the more open lyricism of his earlier verse and gave us, again, several markedly successful poems—"A Light Breather," "Old Lady's Winter Words," and the beautiful "Elegy for Jane." Yet one had a feeling that he was marking time, seeking a new direction.

In *Words for the Wind,* Roethke's collected poems, the new direction appeared. It was a shock. There had been hints that Roethke was interested in Yeats's voice, hints that he might follow the general shift in twentieth-century verse by following wild experimentation with a new formalism. No one could have expected that *Words for the Wind* would contain a series of sixteen "Love Poems" and a sequence, "The Dying Man," all in a voice almost indistinguishable from Yeats's. Roethke, who had invented the most raw and original voice of all our period, was now writing in the voice of another man, and that, perhaps, the most formal and elegant voice of the period.

Yet, also in that book appeared "Meditations of an Old Woman" which suggested still another new direction, and promised, I felt, astonishing new achievements. This poem shows a different influence, but one which seemed much less confining—the Eliot of *Four Quartets.* Perhaps there was also some influence of Richmond Lattimore's translation of *The Iliad:*

> As when silt drifts and sifts down through muddy
>   pond-water,
> Settling in small beads around weeds and sunken branches,
> And one crab, tentative, hunches himself before moving
>   along the bottom,
> Grotesque, awkward, his extended eyes looking at nothing
>   in particular,
> Only a few bubbles loosening from the ill-matched tentacles,
> The tail and smaller legs slipping and sliding slowly
>   backward—
> So the spirit tries for another life,
> Another way and place in which to continue;
> Or a salmon, tired, moving up a shallow stream,
> Nudges into a back-eddy, a sandy inlet,
> Bumping against sticks and bottom-stones, then swinging

> Around, back into the tiny maincurrent, the rush of
>   brownish-white water,
> Still swimming forward—
> So, I suppose, the spirit journeys.

> ("First Meditation")

Here, at any rate, was a language free from the constric-
tions of verse movement, free to use all the cadences of
prose, yet able to collect as much power and authority as
any formal verse:

> I think of the self-involved:
> The ritualists of the mirror, the lonely drinkers,
> The minions of benzedrine and paraldehyde,
> And those who submerge themselves deliberately in trivia,
> Women who become their possessions,
> Shapes stiffening into metal,
> Match-makers, arrangers of picnics—
> What do their lives mean,
> And the lives of their children?—
> The young, brow-beaten early into a baleful silence,
> Frozen by a father's lip, a mother's failure to answer.
> Have they seen, ever, the sharp bones of the poor?
> Or known, once, the soul's authentic hunger,
> Those cat-like immaculate creatures
> For whom the world works?

> ("Fourth Meditation")

Once again, Roethke seemed on the border of a universe of
poetic achievement—a work which might approach the
breadth of Whitman.

Theodore Roethe had died before his next book of poems
appeared. *The Far Field* opens with a poem called "The
Longing" which harks back to those passages in the earlier
book which had promised—both in statement and in vigor
of style—further journeys, new explorations, "All journeys,

I think, are the same: / The movement is forward, after a
few wavers . . . " but now there is a sense of failure, or failure of desire:

> On things asleep, no balm:
> A kingdom of stinks and sighs,
> Fetor of cockroaches, dead fish, petroleum, . . .
> The great trees no longer shimmer;
> Not even the soot dances.
>
> And the spirit fails to move forward,
> But shrinks into a half-life, less than itself,
> Falls back, a slug, a loose worm
> Ready for any crevice,
> An eyeless starer.

That note is struck repeatedly through the "North American Sequence," with which the book opens. Although there
are assertions of new explorations: "I dream of journeys
repeatedly: . . ."

> Old men should be explorers?
> I'll be an Indian.
> Iroquois.

we come away with an opposed sense:

> The self persists like a dying star,
> In sleep, afraid. . . .
>
> I dabble my toes in the brackish foam sliding forward,
> Then retire to a rock higher up on the cliff-side. . . .
>
> The river turns on itself,
> The tree retreats into its own shadow. . . .
>
> I long for the imperishable quiet at the heart of form; . . .

> The lost self changes,
> Turning toward the sea,
> A sea-shape turning around,—
> An old man with his feet before the fire,
> In robes of green, in garments of adieu.

Here, as elsewhere in the book, Roethke accurately predicts his own death, clearly longing for it.

These poems, recording that withdrawal, also, I think, suffer from it. The language grows imprecise with pain, or with growing numbness and half-asleep as an escape from pain. It seems less a regression to capture something and re-create it, than a regression for its own sake, to lose something and uncreate it.

Metrically, too, one has a sense of discouragement and withdrawal. Many of Roethke's earlier cadences are repeated: the whip-cracking of the third book, the easy free verse of the second book. These latter poems—"The Geranium," "The Lizard," "The Meadow Mouse"—are probably the most successful poems in the book. The more ambitious poems seem less successful. This is not to call them failures—they would make a considerable career for many a lesser man. But I, at least, do not feel that they equal Roethke's finest achievements.

What had happened? To investigate that we must go back through Roethke's work and trace out something of his war against form on a different level. And this is a much more causal level—probably causal to Roethke, and certainly causal to the great war against form in our era—the revolt of the sexes against each other and themselves and, in our time, the revolt of the child against the parent. Here, we must investigate not the technical form of Roethke's poems, but rather their statements about his own human form.

Most of Roethke's best earlier poems record a desperate

effort "To be something else, yet still to be!,", to be "somewhere else," to "find the thing he almost was," to be "king
of another condition." As he said it earliest, "I hate my epidermal dress"; as he said it last, "How body from spirit
slowly does unwind / Until we are pure spirit at the end."
We see his struggle against his own form, shape, and size in
all those poems about regression into animal shape—the
sloth, the slug, the insect. Or the continual attempt to lose
his large human form in an identity with *small* forms:

> . . . the little
> Sleepers, numb nudgers in cold dimensions,
> Beetles in caves, newts, stone-deaf fishes,
> Lice tethered to long limp subterranean weeds,
> Squirmers in bogs,
> And bacterial creepers. . . .
>
> ("The Minimal")

This struggle against his own form reached what seemed a
sort of triumph in those journey-poems where he investigat-
ed the landscape as a woman, in the earlier love poems, and
in the numerous poems where he spoke *as* a woman. In the
earlier love poems, he did affirm a shape; not his own, but
the woman's: "She came toward me in the flowing air, / A
shape of change, encircled by its fire," or again: "The
shapes a bright container can contain!" This containment
must have seemed an answer—to lose one's shape, to *be* the
woman through sexual entrance: "Is she what I become? /
Is this my final Face?" and: "I . . . see and suffer myself /
In another being, at last." This idea was repeated over and
over. Yet ecstatic as these poems were, there were two disturbing elements. The woman was not affirmed as herself, a
person in her own right, but rather as a symbol of all being,
or as something the poet might become. And the affirmation
was not made in Roethke's voice, but in Yeats's.

The love poems in the final book are considerably changed. Some ecstasy survives: "Who'd look when he could feel? / She'd more sides than a seal," but even this poem suggests a parting or failure:

> The deep shade gathers night;
> She changed with changing light.
>
> We met to leave again
> That time we broke from time;
> A cold air brought its rain,
> The singing of a stem.
> She sang a final song;
> Light listened when she sang.
>   ("Light Listened")

Here and elsewhere—e.g., "The Long Waters" and "The Sequel"—there seems to be a farewell to that ecstasy, a turning away, or turning inward from the discovery that this could not satisfy the hunger. I do not suggest that any specific love had turned sour or grown cold, but rather that love had perhaps been asked to perform a transformation, to appease a hunger, which no love possibly could satisfy.

What appears dominant in the last book is a desire to escape *all* form and shape, to lose all awareness of otherness, not though entrance to woman as lover, but through re-entrance into eternity conceived as womb, into water as woman, into earth as goddess-mother. This is the burden of "The Long Waters":

> A single wave comes in like the neck of a great swan
> Swimming slowly, its back ruffled by the light cross-winds,
> To a tree lying flat, its crown half broken. . . .
>
> I, who came back from the depths laughing too loudly,
> Become another thing;
> My eyes extend beyond the farthest bloom of the waves;

> I lose and find myself in the long water;
> I am gathered together once more;
> I embrace the world.

and of the "Meditation at Oyster River":

> Now, in this waning of light,
> I rock with the motion of morning;
> In the cradle of all that is,
> I'm lulled into half-sleep
> By the lapping of water,
> Cries of the sandpiper.
> Water's my will, and my way,
> And the spirit runs, intermittently,
> In and out of the small waves, . . .

His new visitant is the child:

> I see in the advancing and retreating waters
> The shape that came from my sleep, weeping:
> The eternal one, the child, the swaying vine branch,
> The numinous ring around the opening flower,
> The friend that runs before me on the windy headlands,
> Neither voice nor vision.
>
> ("The Long Waters")

If, in these last poems, Roethke identifies with an animal, that is only as it tends to represent the child, the baby or fetus. He speaks to "The Lizard":

> He too has eaten well—
> I can see that by the distended pulsing middle;
> And his world and mine are the same,
> The Mediterranean sun shining on us, equally, . . .

and even more, "The Meadow Mouse" which he keeps and treats as, by sympathetic magic, he would be treated:

> Now he's eaten his three kinds of cheese and drunk
>   from his bottle-cap watering-trough—
> So much he just lies in one corner,
> His tail curled under him, his belly big
> As his head; . . .

and when the mouse grows up enough to run away, Roethke sees again his approaching death:

> I think of the nestling fallen into the deep grass,
> The turtle gasping in the dusty rubble of the highway,
> The paralytic stunned in the tub, and the water rising,—
> All things innocent, hapless, forsaken.

In poem after poem, he sees the water rising, the water "moving forward," himself "at a standstill."

This standstill, however, is actively sought and defended. The desire to lose one's own form has taken on a religious rationale to support itself. Where Roethke's earlier free-verse poems were nearly always pure explorations, his more ambitious free-verse poems now try more and more to incorporate a fixed and predetermined religious and irrational certainty:

> Do we move toward God, or merely another condition? . . .

> The shade speaks slowly:
> "Adore and draw near.
> Who knows this—
> Knows all."

("The Abyss")

This is related to the earlier Symbolists' search for a state of being, a religious stasis, as an escape from this world of form and becoming. The poem aims to create a stasis wherein a person is one with all things; that is, where all matter is dissolved. This is related, too, to Roethke's search for pure space as an escape from time. That has been strong in the poems for some time, but now it is easier to see why he identifies space with pure being:

> Space struggled with time;
> The gong of midnight struck
> The naked absolute.
> Sound, silence sang as one.
> ("The Moment")

Our only experience of identity with all space, of omnipresence, is in the womb; our first experience of time brings the mother's breast which may be withdrawn and so force one to recognize external objects, to give up the narcissistic sense of omnipresence and omnipotence, that unity with all objects which Roethke constantly seeks: ". . . the terrible hunger for objects quails me."

This, in turn, helps explain both Roethke's praise of madness (since reason forces the acceptance of external forms and objects) and the poems' increasing mysticism. For instance, in his *New World Writing* remarks on "In a Dark Time," he correctly describes the following as an androgynous act: "The mind enters itself, and God the mind, / And one is One, free in the tearing wind," but also insists that this is a search for God and, moreover, a "dictated" poem. This clarifies, also, the identification of rage with the heart, the true self. Rage is looked upon as a noble quality since it is a rage against the forms of this world, a continued allegiance to one's fantasy of life in the womb.

This intensely creative rejection of form has great destructive possibilities. On the one hand, we have a search for form; on the other (and probably causal to it), a rejection of form which may result in a rejection of all forms, including any form which one might achieve. The balance between these opposed feelings has changed in Roethke's later poems both because of the introduction of borrowed cadences and because of the religious and mystical rationale. Eliot's ideas and Yeats's cadences have rushed in to fill the vacuum of the father-model which could have made this world bearable, yet which Roethke either could not find or could not accept. In one sense, they provide too much form. Roethke's formal poems had always celebrated some kind of lyrical certainty, but that was most frequently a certainty about the nature of one's feelings. Now, rejection of earthly forms has become, itself, a rationale, a convention, a form. As the ideas, the metrical shapes and cadencings all grow firmer, however, the language becomes strangely decayed—or at any rate, fixed and self-imitating. The constant terms of Roethke's earlier poems—the rose, the flame, the shadow, the light, the stalk, the wind—are almost emblems. But as all emblems of an absolute have the same ultimate meaning, so all these terms come more and more to mean the same thing. The words tend to dissolve; the poem is more of a musical rite than a linguistic or dramatic one. That is neither good nor bad in itself, but unless the poem's music is very new and original, a slackness and expectability enters into the poem.

The result here is a little obsessive, like a fantasy. The voice says the same things over and over, always reaching the same predetermined meaning, though with slightly different words each time. But meantime, the voice gets smaller and smaller, like "The phoebe's slow retreating from its song," or like an unhappy child chanting small charms to itself, talking itself to sleep.

But Roethke wrote a book of poems for children—*"I Am!" Says the Lamb*—which appeared in 1961. The first poem in that book is "The Kitty-Cat Bird":

The Kitty-Cat Bird, he sat on a Fence.
Said the Wren, your Song isn't worth 10¢.
You're a Fake, you're a Fraud, you're a Hor-rid Pretense!
   —Said the Wren to the Kitty-Cat Bird.

You've too many Tunes, and none of them Good:
I wish you would act like a bird really should,
Or stay by yourself down deep in the wood,
   —Said the Wren to the Kitty-Cat Bird.

You mew like a Cat, you grate like a Jay:
You squeak like a Mouse that's lost in the Hay,
I wouldn't be You for even a day,
   —Said the Wren to the Kitty-Cat Bird.

The Kitty-Cat Bird, he moped and he cried.
Then a real cat came with a Mouth so Wide,
That the Kitty-Cat Bird just hopped inside;
"At last I'm myself!"—and he up and died
   —Did the Kitty—the Kitty-Cat Bird.

You'd better not laugh; and don't say, "Pooh!"
Until you have thought this Sad Tale through:
Be sure that whatever you are is you
   —Or you'll end like the Kitty-Cat Bird.

I wonder how many lovers of Roethke's poetry have read
that to their children, perhaps at bedtime, unsuspecting of
its horrors? Or of its prophecy? Who could have guessed
that Roethke—who meant so much to us—could think so
badly of himself? Or might issue a warning to the children
which he himself was unable to heed?

But that is too fearsome a place to end an essay. Earlier,
Roethke gave us another animal picture of himself, of his
certainties, and of his journey into sleep—"The Sloth":

In moving-slow he has no Peer.
You ask him something in his Ear;
He thinks about it for a Year;

And, then, before he says a Word
There, upside down (unlike a Bird),
He will assume that you have Heard—

A most Ex-as-per-at-ing Lug.
But should you call his manner Smug,
He'll sigh and give his Branch a Hug;

Then off again to Sleep he goes,
Still swaying gently by his Toes,
And you just *know* he knows he knows.

Perhaps he does. Surely, after enduring so much uncertainty and anguish, he *deserves* to know. After offering so much for *our* knowledge, he deserves to sleep well.

FREDERICK J. HOFFMAN

Theodore Roethke
The Poetic Shape of Death

HE POETRY OF THEODORE ROETHKE DESCRIBES FOUR stages in the development of what he intended it to say. While this may not be a sensational truth, the intensity with which Roethke engages in each of the stages marks both it and him as exceptional. From the second volume (*The Lost Son*) on, Roethke made his verse his own, inscribed it with the signature of his inimitable temperament and fancy.

We might as well define these stages at the very beginning: they relate to a prenatal condition, to childhood, to the move toward maturity, and to the contemplation of the conditions and implications of death. Throughout, there is an overlapping of one upon the other, a spiral turning back, a reach for self-definition. More than normally, Roethke was overtaken by the fancies of childhood and by the fear of being forced out of that state, with no reliable surrogates for "papa" and "mama." The poems therefore abound in talk comparable to a semi-intelligible child's garble, a language in itself designed to induce security (because of its identification with a time when he *was* secure):

Mips and ma the mooly moo,
The likes of him is biting who,
A cow's a care and who's a coo?—
What footie does is final.

My dearest dear my fairest fair,
Your father tossed a cat in air,
Though neither you nor I was there,—
What footie does is final.

Be large as an owl, be slick as a frog,
Be good as a goose, be big as a dog,
Be sleek as a heifer, be long as a hog,—
What footie will do will be final.
                    ("Praise to the End!")

Roethke's poetry is one of the most exhaustive, vital, and vivid reports we have of a soul in the several agonies normally recorded in one human life. The intensity results from an absorption in a form of subliminal nature, a deep sense of the most elementary agonies attending the process and the necessity of living. But it has other causes as well. Roethke impressed both his friends and readers profoundly as a human being, almost overwhelmingly "present," in his person as in his poetry. When I saw him in the summer of 1957, I had been teaching a seminar at the University of Washington on the subject that led to the publication of *The Mortal No.* He told me then that he was much concerned with the mysteries and paradoxes of death, and that his new poetry reflected these concerns. It did just that; and the meditative poems that appeared in *Words for the Wind* and, recently, in *The Far Field,* demonstrate this interest remarkably. Nowhere in modern American poetry are the metaphysically speculative and the naturally commonplace so well balanced, so reciprocal in effect.

I want especially to notice these two aspects of Roethke's

verse: the "metaphysical fusion" I have spoken of and the
effect upon it of the puzzle of death—not so much the expectation of it, but the exhausting contemplation of its curious nature and the struggle to define it in public terms.

Roethke was at the beginning so engrossed with the wonder of his origins—and of the origins of life—that his poetry
described a spiral of flight, fear, and return; the place itself
can be characterized as the condition of "underness," which
exists "everywhere." In *Open House* (more formally written
and imitative than his other work) there is little we may call
characteristic of Roethke. Like most first volumes, it offers
only clues as to his future direction, though it scarcely even
serves for this purpose. Like a hundred others, the poem
"Death Piece" states a general condition of insentience,
without localizing it or investing it with emotional energy:

> Invention sleeps within a skull
> No longer quick with light,
> The hive that hummed in every cell
> Is now sealed honey-tight.
>
> His thought is tied, the curving prow
> Of motion moored to rock;
> And minutes burst upon a brow
> Insentient to shock.

Only with *The Lost Son* were his characteristic rhetorical
gestures revealed. These have, of course, been much discussed: as a "peculiar balance of the natural and the artificial . . .";[1] as describing the "agony of coming alive, the painful miracle of growth . . .";[2] as a form of "Noh" monologue,

[1] Kenneth Burke, "The Vegetal Radicalism of Theodore Roethke," *Sewanee Review*, LVI (Winter, 1950), 82.
[2] Stanley Kunitz, "News of the Root," *Poetry*, LXXIII (January, 1949), 225.

in which, "wearing a mask painted with a fixed smile of pain, he visits a pond in a wood which is haunted by a nymph-like ghost, and performs a very slow and solemn pirouetting dance, . . ."[3]

Of course, the greenhouse provides the scene and source of all the poems in this volume, and of many others. Roethke shows a remarkable awareness of the scene, as well as a sensitivity to its every conceivable affective meaning. He always reacts precisely and meaningfully to it, as a person deeply committed to it in memory and making it the basis of all meditations. The greenhouse has a peculiar usefulness as a microcosm of subhuman life. Within its vivid forms, a number of effects reside: the specially created climatic conditions, the *schwärmerei* of plant life awaiting the "knock" of attention and the flow of warmth which help their growth, and the artificially created "edenic" conditions which guarantee that freshness, beauty, and purity (the rose, the carnation) will survive.

Most of all, the image of "papa" dominates:

> That hump of a man bunching chrysanthemums
> Or pinching-back asters, or planting azaleas,
> Tamping and stamping dirt into pots,—
> ("Old Florist")

As God, "papa" gives life and endows it with order, separating the good from the expendable nongood, "weeding" impurities from this floral Eden:

> Pipe-knock.

> Scurry of warm over small plants.
> Ordnung! Ordnung!
> Papa is coming!

[3] Stephen Spender, "Words for the Wind," *New Republic*, CXLI (Aug. 10, 1959), 22.

A fine haze moved over the leaves;
Frost melted on far panes;
The rose, the chrysanthemum turned toward the light.
Even the hushed forms, the bent yellowy weeds
Moved in a slow up-sway.

("The Return")

Roethke believed the "papa principle" to be indispensable to a forthgoing knowledge. Many of the poems in the volumes beginning with *The Lost Son* characteristically struggle to escape the "slime," the "loam," the level of pre-natal existence; in short, they offer a portrayal of what Roethke called "an effort to be born, and later, to become something more."[4] Both being born and becoming "something more" are disturbed by the agonies of self-assertion, and of separating the self from its prenatal associations. The language at this point is almost without abstraction, as indeed that of a small child is: full of long vowel sounds, one-syllabled words which label, questions for which there seems to be no answer. But the poems show a progression nevertheless. Roethke spoke of the need "first to go back," in order eventually to go forward ("Open Letter," p. 69). The poems move chiefly from dark (the "underness" that exists everywhere) to light: or, from the dark recesses of the almost entirely quiescent self, to the world where the light requires an activity of the mind, what he called "spirit" or "soul."

The basic natural origin is defined in terms of "Shoots dangled and drooped, / Lolling obscenely from mildewed crates"; "Even the dirt kept breathing a small breath." The leaf gives us a primary natural image of life; extended, it suggests the hand, and when the body dies, the hand has the appearance of a leaf deprived of its source of life. This dep-

---

[4] "Open Letter," in *Mid-Century American Poets,* ed. John Ciardi (New York: Twayne, 1950), p. 68.

rivation resembles the kind of separation suffered by a leaf cut away from its tree, a flower taken from its sustaining soil. The title poem of *The Lost Son* describes the full experience of struggling to be—in this case, to be born, then to be, then simply once again to return to the being of the nearly born. The imagery describes the fear which accompanies the spiral movement; the agony of Part One is described in terms of a "going forth" in doubt and fear, like the birth of any organic being. The "under" side demonstrates its reality even more powerfully and persuasively than the outside.

> Where do the roots go?
>   Look down under the leaves.
> Who put the moss there?
>   These stones have been here too long.
> Who stunned the dirt into noise?
>   Ask the mole, he knows.
> I feel the slime of a wet nest.
>   Beware Mother Mildew.
> Nibble again, fish nerves.
>
> ("The Pit")

But, along with these apparently simple queries, the poet suggests a growing awareness of the outer world. We stand "out there" when we look back upon the minimal life we have left. Ultimately, Roethke's protagonist (his "I," who comes very close to being himself) sees the natural world formally, as in the beginning of winter, when we so often acutely sense the quality of forms and surfaces, since the "underness" is quieted.

> Light traveled over the field;
> Stayed.
> The weeds stopped swinging.
> The mind moved, not alone,

> Through the clear air, in the silence.
> ("It was beginning winter.")

In time, this condition of silence will become symbolically contained, like and yet very different from the various still-nesses of T. S. Eliot's *Four Quartets*. Roethke's achievements of silence always indicate a move out of the noise, the thickness, the confusion of life (or a meaningful pause in it), while Eliot's seem forever to dominate life and to force it into a subsidiary and symbolic *ménage*.

These movements occur in much of Roethke's verse: the move outward ("Mother me out of here . . ."); the desire to return, for reinforcing sustenance, the occasional sense of quiet "at the centre" ("A rose sways least. / The redeemer comes a dark way."), and not always, but with increasing frequency—a feeling of perfection, in which the noise of living lessens and one may contemplate the condition of life as a symbolically "free" condition:

> To know that light falls and fills, often without our knowing,
> As an opaque vase fills to the brim from a quick pouring,
> Fills and trembles at the edge yet does not flow over,
> Still holding and feeding the stem of the contained flower.
> ("The Shape of the Fire")

The movement in Roethke's verse becomes more complicated, as the poetry itself becomes more meditative, more "metaphysically extended." It reaches out beyond the greenhouse world, but always with a sense of the need to return. *Praise to the End!* reminds us of the full cycle. Roethke's mind and sensibility were formed by the greenhouse experience, and most of his poems remind us of the poet's memories. He chose the title of his next book not so much to call our attention to Wordsworth's view of nature

as to emphasize his own uniquely separate position. I cite
enough lines from the 1805-6 version of *The Prelude* to give
some sense of the strange relationship:

> ... Praise to the end!
> Thanks likewise for the means! But I believe
> That Nature, oftentimes, when she would frame
> A favor'd Being, from his earliest dawn
> Of infancy doth open out the clouds,
> As at the touch of lightning, seeking him
> With gentlest visitation; not the less,
> Though haply aiming at the self-same end,
> Does it delight her sometimes to employ
> Severer interventions, ministry
> More palpable, and so she dealt with me.

The phrase which begins this quotation denotes a happy
gratification over the sense of being that Wordsworth enjoys
through the act of Nature upon his being; he is surprised
that he should have "come through" so well, that the fears
he suffered in the past should have anything to do with the
making of "The calm existence that is mine when I / Am
worthy of myself! . . ."[5] In one sense, Roethke's use of the
phrase suggests a stage in his growth, though his sense of
nature strikes us as far more "intimate," direct, and imagistic than Wordsworth's. The formalities of Roethke's verse
and attitude, however, did increase with the publication of
Praise to the End![6] He was more and more drawn to a con-
sideration of "last things," and the title phrase (as did
Wordsworth's use of it) expressed surprise that nature
should have permitted him to meditate about them seriously.

[5] William Wordsworth, *The Prelude*, ed. Ernest de Selincourt and Helen
Darbishire (Oxford: Clarendon Press, 1959), p. 22.
[6] I do not mean that the verse became "classical." If anything, the use
of the free line, controlled almost invariably by either end punctuation
or caesural pause, increased; and the characteristic vigor remained much
in evidence.

The verse bespeaks a genuine maturing. Beginning with *Praise,* Roethke followed the practice of combining selections from earlier volumes with new poems, to suggest the spiral or cyclic progression he had mentioned in his "Open Letter." But "progress" showed more obviously in the new poems, and the quality of memory changed. With the death of "papa" ("He was all whitey bones / And skin like paper"), a change occurred in the image of Godhood ("God's somewhere else"), which came more and more closely to resemble an independent self ("I'm somebody else now"). The responsibilities of the new self are seen everywhere. The echoes of childhood phrases slowly give way to the need of being—without regret—independently oneself. "There's no alas / Where I live" recalls the blessed simplicities of a childhood he finds it hard to give up. But the image of himself as "standing up" and alone ("When I stand, I'm almost a tree") appears more frequently than before. He defines himself in the new status through many devices:

> We'll be at the business of what might be
> Looking toward what we are. . . .
>
> I've played with the fishes
> Among the unwrinkling ferns
> In the wake of a ship of wind;
> But now the instant ages,
> And my thought hunts another body.
> ("Give Way, Ye Gates")

The other body offers both another meaning of self and another self. Roethke is involved both in his own maturing and in his finding another person, whose love will illuminate his own identity. His Dante must also know a Beatrice. He needs to take a long and fearsome journey to "somewhere else," but he is willing to assume the risks.

> Has the dark a door?
> I'm somewhere else,—
> I insist!
> I am.
> ("Sensibility! O La!")

"Praise to the End!" provides an especially revealing and significant statement of his new role, his "progress." The elements of nature (not Wordsworth's respected, capitalized Nature) remain, as do the childish sounds (moo—who—coo; frog—dog—hog); but the poet speaks mainly of the need to "separate": "I conclude! I conclude! / My dearest dust, I can't stay here." In his escape from the "under world of the greenhouse, the poet retains the belief the natural world has given him. But he is also aware of the crisis of separation, the threat to childhood security:

> I have been somewhere else; I remember the sea-faced uncles.
> I hear, clearly, the heart of another singing,
> Lighter than bells,
> Softer than water.

The experience with nature now demands a transition to "somewhere else." "I can't crawl back through those veins, / I ache for another choice." Roethke calls to the small things of his past, to "sing" as symbols. Nature must become "A house for wisdom; a field for revelation." He has, in other words, found the need for other meanings, for ways of defining himself through others than "papa," in a world wider than Woodlawn.

The poet needs also to find another vocabulary, to reinforce the old one. The respect for life remains, but he approaches it obliquely, sometimes even with the aid of "literary" and "metaphysical" reflections. The famous sequence, "Four for Sir John Davies," refers to a sixteenth-century

English poet, whose Spenserian poem, "Orchestra" (1596), attempts to present nature in a universal dance, or a solemn, orderly motion.[7] The importance of the sequence depends primarily upon its full commitment to sexual involvement. Roethke sees the sexual act as both a move away from the simplicities of childish "aloneness" and "an harmonious" recovery of life. The third step is now achieved. The poet sees love at the moment as not wearisome but rich in pleasure and delights. Moreover, we are aware of a "standing with" —a dancing with, a partnership. The "I" changes to "we" in this maneuver; the delights are not unmixed with doubt and wonder, but they seem to be a profitable means of sending the self toward that "somewhere else" that Roethke had earlier called "far away."

> Incomprehensible gaiety and dread
> Attended what we did. Behind, before,
> Lay all the lonely pastures of the dead;
> The spirit and the flesh cried out for more.
> We two, together, on a darkening day
> Took arms against our own obscurity.
>   ("The Wraith")

Roethke uses a new vocabulary, even a newly formal verse pattern. The end pauses usually remain; but, the idea being more complex, the phrase which includes it enlarges. For at least a moment in his time, he pauses to speculate upon love, as later he will meditate upon dying, in the fashion of the modern "metaphysical poet," a John Crowe Ransom, probably more than an Allen Tate. Having chosen "desire" as a device for extending the range of self-definition, he must now define the word and overcome his doubts concerning its value. It is scarcely reassuring to know that "two" are more than "one" in the effort to shut out "our

---

[7] See Ralph Mills, *Theodore Roethke* (Minneapolis: University of Minnesota Press, 1963), pp. 31-35, for a discussion of this indebtedness.

own obscurity," unless the "two" can become permanently a One in the economy of life. Beyond the dissolution of the two lies death; the danger of annihilation is already genuinely present, even in the most pleasant conditions. At least momentarily the union seems to hold:

> Did each become the other in that play?
> She laughed me out, and then she laughed me in;
> In the deep middle of ourselves we lay; . . .

The fourth poem of the sequence speaks even more confidently of the ministering effectiveness of love. Speaking of Dante's being blinded by the inner light of the Paradiso, Roethke defines it as the light of love, reducing it to love itself and to the verbal trickeries by which it is embellished and exalted. "All lovers live by longing, and endure: / Summon a vision and declare it pure."

The lovers "undid chaos to a curious sound"; the "I" of Roethke's world hopes now to give "thought" to "things," to work on the assumption that "We think by feeling . . .": that is, that we endow things, and acts, with ideal virtues by living and feeling them (or, by acting in a "necessary conjunction," in the spirit of Eliot's "East Coker").

Love assists in our fight to postpone death; it is also a testimony of Godhood. As a form of dying, love at least momentarily pushes the threat of dying out of mind. The protagonist concludes the *Waking* volume in a simple, calm assertion.

> Light takes the Tree; but who can tell us how?
> The lowly worm climbs up a winding stair;
> I wake to sleep, and take my waking slow.
>   ("The Waking")

Love remains an important human gesture in *Words for the Wind*. The lover speaks again and again of the newly

achieved confidence his love has given him. His cries are no
longer prompted by fear, but by delight: ". . . I know /
The root, the core of a cry." The title poem, from which this
quotation comes, continues in a mood of frankly innocent
confidence:

> I kiss her moving mouth,
> Her swart hilarious skin;
> She breaks my breath in half;
> She frolics like a beast;
> And I dance round and round,
> A fond and foolish man,
> And see and suffer myself
> In another being, at last.

The open sensuality remains a prominent element in the wit
of "I Knew a Woman":

> She was the sickle; I, poor I, the rake,
> Coming behind her for her pretty sake
> (But what prodigious mowing we did make).

The thought of death is not precluded by the performance
of love; it is only postponed, if even that. The sacrifice of
the self to another yields much pleasure; but the Roethkean
"I" eventually allows death to intrude: at first, by recon-
verting what was once a pure pleasure into a human gesture
of dubious value. "The Sensualists" suggest a surfeit of
love—in other words, the conclusion that it cannot always,
entirely, put aside the thought of death. The lovers are, in
fact, like Ransom's of "The Equilibrists," doomed to live in
a prison of their love:

> "The bed itself begins to quake,
>   I hate this sensual pen;
> My neck, if not my heart, will break
>   If we do this again,"—

> Then each fell back, limp as a sack,
> Into the world of men.

With the apparent failure of love, the old questions return; only, now they seem more importunate, and the answers cannot be disguised in sentiment or in fantasy. Loving offers the last barrier to the thought of dying. The protagonist more than ever despairs of his power to define life and himself; he needs to do the first to prepare for death, the second in order personally to bear it. His thoughts return briefly to "papa"; his intellect inquires if "form" will help to limit himself. "Papa" had once been sufficient to pull the weeds from what the poet as God principle had wanted to survive. Now Roethke's "I" needs some formal way of saving himself from sensual chaos:

> I know I love, yet know not where I am;
> I paw the dark, the shifting midnight air.
> Will the self, lost, be found again? In form?
> I walk the night to keep my five wits warm.
>   ("The Renewal")

Such a failure should now appear inevitable, a consequence of the physical circumstances of love. For, in the true "metaphysical" consensus of love, the individual dying was always associated with the final thrust of death, as in John Donne's "Canonization" ode. But in Roethke's poems the particulars of love are almost always linked to the past: to the warm, moist, subliminal world of the womb that sponsored all living and the "papa" who sustained it. He can only cry, "Father, I'm far from home, / And I have gone nowhere," and "I fear for my own joy." The failure is accompanied by the recurring imagery of the past and by the son's renewed fears. Father had been "Father of flowers"; but the son combines "several selves" which reflect at first

"Lewd, tiny, careless lives / That scuttled under stones,"
and he eventually becomes "myself, alone."

He has finally to persuade himself of death. The poem
"The Dying Man" is dedicated to Yeats, but actually the
Roethke persona looks firmly at "Death's possibilities."
Now, he sees dying as a continual becoming; this knowledge, of growth as a move toward mortality, is indispensable
to the adjustment. The great poem of *Words,* "Meditations
of an Old Woman," combines gracefully and skillfully the
two vocabularies Roethke had developed, the "natural" and
the "metaphysical." Once again, "The weeds hiss at the edge
of the field"; but the old woman can no longer claim a su-
periority to the small natural particulars (when they do not
frighten her, they bore her):

> I've become a strange piece of flesh,
> Nervous and cold, bird-furtive, whiskery,
> With a cheek soft as a hound's ear.
> What's left is light as a seed;
> I need an old crone's knowing.
> ("First Meditation")

This remarkable poem admits all types of encounter with
mortality. The old woman, on the edge of death, has only
her "meditations" to help her tolerate the expectation. She
must, finally, learn to "sit still," in the spirit of Eliot's
"Ash-Wednesday," but without theological assurances.
For, in her extremity, she must seek in the familiar details of
nature the substitute for a god. "In such times," she says,
thinking of the sights and smells and sounds of her past life,
"lacking a god, / I am still happy." Yet she finds it difficult
to speak of a soul, because in Roethke the soul must always
somehow be activated; it cannot rest merely on a theological
premise.

> The soul knows not what to believe,
> In its small folds, stirring sluggishly,
> In the least place of its life,
> A pulse beyond nothingness,
> A fearful ignorance.[8]
>   ("What Can I Tell My Bones?")

In the end, the old woman lives only in dread of the rational view of death, and hopes that she may find some escape from its implications.

> I rock in my own dark,
> Thinking, God has need of me.
> The dead love the unborn.
>   ("What Can I Tell My Bones?")

She expresses a sense of renewal in her final observations: as though nature will reclaim her in allowing others to be born, as though she were for a valiant moment, "Anna Livia Plurabelle." Roethke is a poet who finds it unimaginable to rest with any large denial of life.

The Far Field demonstrates the extent to which Roethke had defined death to himself before the summer of 1963. The poems, or some of them, also testify to the agony of moving toward the threshold of death. I do not mean to say that the thought of death was constantly with him, but only that he suffered a type of "dark night" and that it was partly caused by his being unable to will a transcendence that he could also will to believe in. The "congress of stinks" of *The Lost Son* here becomes

[8] Ultimately, in these "Meditations," Roethke arrives at the biblical phrase, "Do these bones live?" which Eliot made prominent in Part Two of "Ash-Wednesday." Roethke's woman is concerned not so much with the promise of resurrection which they originally suggested but rather with the old woman's power to speak *to* them. The title of this, the last section of the long poem, is "What Can I Tell My Bones?"

> A kingdom of stinks and sighs,
> Fetor of cockroaches, dead fish, petroleum,
> Worse than castoreum of mink or weasels,
> Saliva dripping from warm microphones,
> Agony of crucifixion on barstools.
>   ("The Longing")

There is reason to believe that Roethke suffered these agonies because (1) the world of "papa" no longer enlightened or assured him; and (2) he failed to secure consolation in the pleasures of what he called ". . . the imperishable quiet at the heart of form." But I also suspect that, occasionally at least, he saw—perhaps forced himself to see—the possibility of the flesh's assuming the role of the spirit. The image of water, which in *The Lost Son* was made equivalent to "Money money money," now more frequently takes on the conventional symbolic aspects of death and the soul:

> Water's my will, and my way,
> And the spirit runs, intermittently,
> In and out of the small waves,
> Runs with the intrepid shorebirds—
> How graceful the small before danger!
>   ("Meditation at Oyster River")

However improvised this metaphor appears to be, it will certainly play an important role in the ultimate critical assessment of Roethke's work. With much of the evidence in, he appears to me to have alternated between the fear of death which his doubt of immortality forced upon him, and the speculative pleasure in his own power of transcendence. I do not think this is an "aesthetic" power solely, or entirely, because much of the prospect of transcendence had to be willed; that is, his pleasure in the metaphors of transcendence undoubtedly were earned by a strong effort of the will.[9]

Ultimately, Roethke seems to have come back to a peculiarly American "stance," the Emersonian confidence in *seeing* the spirit in matter, also, in a sense, in *creating* matter (or forming it) through the power of the transcending will. Much more than Emerson's,[10] Roethke's mind was drenched in particulars. He had at the beginning to move away from them, in order to notice his own identity, to "be himself." The "papa" principle had eventually to yield to the search for adequate limits of self, simply because "papa" had died. Momentarily, he found a surrogate definition in the physical nature of love; when his confidence in this ceased, he was forced alternately to meditate upon the end of a temporal process and to will transcendence of it.

"In a Dark Time" illustrates the conditions persuasively. The "dark time" has several applications: to the darkness of "underness" which he found everywhere; to the darkness of despair that came to him when he found that he had alone both to define and to defend himself; and, of course, to the time of death, of what he calls "the deepening shade" and "the echoing wood." He conceives of himself as both creating (as in the poem) and living in the world of nature.

[9] I should maintain this despite his statement that the last two lines of "In a Dark Time" were the product of pure inspiration. "This was a dictated poem," he said in 1961, "something given, scarcely mine at all. For about three days before its writing I felt disembodied, out of time; then the poem virtually wrote itself, on a day in summer, 1958." "The Poet and His Critics," ed. Anthony Ostroff, *New World Writing*, XIX (1961), 214.

[10] Whom he might well have had in mind when he wrote "Prayer Before Study":

> A fool can play at being solemn
> Revolving on his spinal column.
>
> Deliver me, O Lord, from all
> Activity centripetal.

Such a union of living and "making live" may surely be con-
sidered an act of voluntary creativity, in which the creator
exists, surrounded by his creatures; the latter survive partly
in his memory, but are refined in his having remembered
them. As he has said in his "comment," the heron and the
wren, the "beasts of the hill and serpents of the den," ought
not to be thought of as either emblematic or strange, but
rather as a part of his own experience. One may do too much
by way of endowing Roethke as a "son of Blake," or of
Yeats, or whomever.

The "madness" is a condition of the soul. One nurses his
idiosyncrasies at his own peril, but there is nothing "mad"
about his accommodation to the fact and the necessities of
"the dark time." He is on the "edge" of meaning, looks out
upon "that place among the rocks. . . ." Naturally, in consequence of the evidence we have already examined, he is as-
saulted by, not only a "congress of stinks," but "A steady
storm of correspondences!" These are not unlike Baudelaire's "vivants piliers," which "Laissent parfois sortir de
confuses paroles"; but Roethke does not want to be thought
either "theoretical" or pompous about them. In fact, the
analogical necessity is derived not from them in themselves,
but from his need to stand apart from them and to strength-
en both his facility of inference and his power of implication.

Ultimately, the issue becomes one of maneuvering within
the circumstances of his mortality.

> A man goes far to find out what he is—
> Death of the self in a long, tearless night,
> All natural shapes blazing unnatural light.

The beautiful simplicity of these lines is convincing because
they come at the end of a long career of defining self, a time
during which the quest of the "I" has been dramatized bril-
liantly again and again. But the poet indicates not only a

quest for "self-definition," despite the question, "Which I is *I?*" He as much strives to escape the multiplicity of selves, the "storm of correspondences," as he does to steady himself for the prospect that *all* selves disintegrate, that death happens to all of them.

So, we have the brilliant final stanza, with its quizzicality of Emily Dickinson ("My soul, like some heat-maddened summer fly, / Keeps buzzing at the sill. . . ."), and its apparent Emersonian affirmation:

> A fallen man, I climb out of my fear.
> The mind enters itself, and God the mind,
> And one is One, free in the tearing wind.

As Roethke has said, these lines are far from the forced improvisation they have been accused of being:

The moment before Nothingness, before near annihilation, the moment of supreme disgust is the worst: when change comes it is either total loss of consciousness—symbolical or literal death—*or* a quick break into another state, not necessarily serene, but frequently a bright blaze of consciousness that translates itself into action.[11]

The "fallen man" is the self that has gone the long way toward deprivation; he recalls not only "the lost son," but the son of a dead father, and he must therefore find a way of making significant use of himself. He climbs "out of [his] fear," in the manner that we have watched so often in Roethke's books. He is that loathsome thing, the fly, what he has called "a disease-laden, heat-maddened fly—to me a more intolerable thing than a rat" ("The Poet . . . ," p. 217). Surely no one will hesitate to grant him the choice. In any case, the fly is Emily Dickinson's only in *being* a fly; for her the insect is not loathsome because it serves as the décor of mortality.

[11] "The Poet and His Critics," pp. 217-18.

If we grant Roethke the right to his first metaphors, we find it difficult not to permit him the concluding ones—despite the fact that these are more suddenly (or at least, more unexpectedly) grasped. The mind's entering itself seems to me to be Roethke's steady concern. Far from a solipsistic condition, or a madly egocentric one, what we have is the process of self-examination which all of us come to when we need to "stand aside," when we abandon the "papa principle" or it abandons us. We are less certain that God enters the mind. Roethke points out that God is not customarily supposed, by the "hot-gospelers," to enter the mind, but rather invades the heart.

In any case, the final line offers a neat possibility: if, after God enters the mind (not the heart or the liver, or even the soul), "one is One," then we may assume that the mind (with the help of God, perhaps) changes the "one" to the "One." To conceive of this change requires both creative ingenuity and daring. For the soul is "free in the tearing wind," and this freedom can scarcely be envied or ideally desired.

At least in terms of the evidence, Roethke has come the long way, to climb out of both his fear of chaos and his trust in easy and comfortable confidences, and to stand in the place of "papa," ministering not so much to the many as to the One he has himself created. Perhaps the idea strikes us as fanciful; but one can, I am sure, be too much handicapped by logical or even eschatological necessity, to see the neatness and convincingness with which "In a Dark Time" stands as a genuine resolution of the mazes caused by life and the problems created by the expectation of death. Roethke's death, seen in the light of this *mort accomplie,* most properly sets the seal to his life, in terms of the imaginative brilliance and the moral courage which dominate and direct his poetry.

RALPH J. MILLS, JR.

In the Way of Becoming Roethke's Last Poems

THE PRIMARY THEMATIC CONCERN IN THEODORE Roethke's poetry is with the evolution and identity of the self, its beginnings with an individual's birth, its organic growth which resembles the growth of things in nature, and its attainment of a maturity and independence that bring it into a new, harmonious relationship with creation.[1] I want to call attention here to the different phases of the self's evolution as we find them treated in the last poems of *The Far Field,* especially in those two parts of the book called "North American Sequence" and "Sequence, Sometimes Metaphysical" in which the poet exceeds the limits of previous development and sets forth on an arduous but successful quest for mystical illumination.

This undertaking, as we shall see more concretely in the poems themselves, requires a moral or spiritual trimming, a divesting of self which cannot be accomplished in one gesture, and which, though it might at first appear so, is not a

---

[1] That relationship is extended and deepened in the love lyrics, where cosmic resonances are sounded by the sensual and spiritual exchange between poet and beloved. These matters I have discussed in more detail in *Theodore Roethke* (Minneapolis: University of Minnesota Press, 1963).

reversal of the process of growth in the self that occupies so much of Roethke's earlier work. It is, rather, evidence of the genuine fulfillment of that process and brings the body of his art to a strong and moving completion. Such poems of supernatural consciousness are anyway not without precedent in Roethke's writing; indeed, they are prepared for by many poems in the second half of *Words for the Wind* and by a consistent use of certain metaphors and types of imagery to designate the operations of the inner life. Then, too, in manner the poems of "North American Sequence" derive from techniques put to work in previous poems of psychic growth in *The Lost Son* and *Praise to the End!,* as well as from those of the later "Meditations of an Old Woman," while the closing "Sequence, Sometimes Metaphysical" recalls Roethke's predilection for a taut, economical lyricism which he continued to practice throughout his career. Thus the two sequences emphasize the main tendencies of his poetic manner—the one freer, Whitmanesque at times, answering his demands for "the breath unit, the language that is natural to the immediate thing," "the catalogue," and "the eye close on the object"[2]—the other constructed along more traditional lines, capable of containing and concentrating immense pressures of feeling. These manners are most appropriate to the use Roethke makes of them in *The Far Field:* the long, free, variable lines of "North American Sequence" carry the burden of natural and geographical detail, the experience of the outer world of nature, of creatures and things that is intimately related to the poet's states of consciousness, their rising and falling, their stillness and motion; the spare, and more formal, character of the lyrics in "Sequence, Sometimes Metaphysical" parallels the further stage of visionary experience they embody, for at this point the focus of activity is almost entirely inward or spirit-

---

[2] "Some Remarks on Rhythm," *Poetry,* XCVII (October, 1960), 45.

ual and considerations of external reality are, at best, secondary.

Within the evolutionary scheme of Roethke's poetry, the scheme which traces the course of the emergent self, there is a simultaneous development of what is variously called soul or spirit, which we might say is the inner or ruling principle of the self. The term "self" appears to embrace and unite both the physical and spiritual components of the individual into a whole of particular identity. The spirit is perhaps the bloom, the last and highest glory of the self and so becomes the guiding and motivating principle in its experience, its ascent on the scale of being. Roethke portrays it similarly in "A Light Breather" and indicates connections between his title and traditional associations of breath and wind with spirit:

> The spirit moves,
> Yet stays:
> Stirs as a blossom stirs,
> Still wet from its bud-sheath,
> Slowly unfolding,
> Turning in the light with its tendrils;
> Plays as a minnow plays,
> Tethered to a limp weed, swinging,
> Tail around, nosing in and out of the current,
> Its shadows loose, a watery finger;
> Moves, like the snail,
> Still inward,
> Taking and embracing its surroundings,
> Never wishing itself away,
> Unafraid of what it is,
> A music in a hood,
> A small thing,
> Singing.

This brief poem holds the implications for the spiritual journey out of the self which begins in an organized way with

"North American Sequence." The spirit as essence of the
organic self seeks finally to go beyond that self's circumference. What Roethke tells us in the first two lines above is
revealed many times over in his later work: the spirit retains its central position and yet seems to step outside itself,
to merge with things other than itself. Thus the spirit is
fluid, can expand indefinitely, a potentiality that is fundamental to mystical experience. But this expansion is not new
to Roethke's poetry; here are two examples from *Words for
the Wind:*

> I know the motion of the deepest stone.
> Each one's himself, yet each one's everyone.
> ("The Sententious Man")

> Dry bones! Dry bones! I find my loving heart,
> Illumination brought to such a pitch
> I see the rubblestones begin to stretch
> As if reality had split apart
> And the whole motion of the soul lay bare:
> I find that love, and I am everywhere.
> ("The Renewal")

These extreme moments vividly demonstrate the kind of
experience implicit in "A Light Breather" and also qualify
as illustrations of the earlier stages of mystical awakening.
But such positive instances, leading the way to greater visionary knowledge, do not continue unimpeded; there are
occasions of spiritual setback constantly to be faced, with
their nearly overwhelming atmosphere of negation, nothingness, a terrible human desolation. In " 'The Shimmer of
Evil' " the poet, and all creatures and things, remain impris-
oned in their selfhood; everything loses its depth and lumi-
nosity and shows only hard, impenetrable surfaces which
forbid communion and force the poet back into himself; the
spirit, to borrow Roethkean metaphors, back into its sheath

or shell: ". . . and I was only I. / —There was no light; there was no light at all. . . ."

One could multiply examples of this sort; even poems like "The Lost Son" display the delays and retreats of the self as well as its forward movements. But in the last poems, where the intention to achieve mystical illumination is more sustained, this negative experience becomes more terrifying and, if it is possible, more purposive. Among the pieces from *Words for the Wind* depicting negative spiritual states of lassitude, guilt, and deprivation, I think not only of " 'The Shimmer of Evil' " but "Elegy," "The Beast," "The Song," and particularly "The Exorcism," in which the poet undergoes a frightening purgation. Self-questioning and interior stagnation haunt the reflective consciousness of the speaker in "Meditations of an Old Woman"; she fluctuates between ecstasy (a sense of harmony with creation) and periods of dryness (failures of vision), such as provide the ground rhythm of "North American Sequence." "By dying daily, I have come to be," writes Roethke in the fourth poem of "The Dying Man," and this alternation between contrary states is the basic pattern of experience on the path to intensifying mystical perception. Evelyn Underhill says:

We are to expect, then, as part of the condition under which human consciousness appears to work, that for every affirmation of the mystic life there will be a negation waiting for the unstable self. Progress in contemplation, for instance, is marked by just such an alternation between light and shade: at first between "consolation" and aridity; then between "dark contemplation" and sharp intuitions of Reality . . . each joyous ecstasy entails a painful or negative ecstasy. The states of darkness and illumination coexist over a long period, alternating sharply and rapidly.[3]

True to his personal experience and to his insight, Roethke carries these "states of darkness and illumination"

[3] *Mysticism* (New York: Meridian Books, 1955), p. 383.

into the midst of his poetic work, where, as we have noted, they fall quite readily into its course of development. In *The Far Field* he begins to purify and purge himself as he aims toward a union with or experience of the Divine; that process reaches its zenith in the lyrics of "Sequence, Sometimes Metaphysical."

Appropriately enough, "North American Sequence" begins in a condition of spiritual emptiness and torpor. The poet is at the nadir, sunk in a world of the senses, tormented by a hypersensitive awareness of physical and moral decay:[4]

> On things asleep, no balm:
> A kingdom of stinks and sighs,
> Fetor of cockroaches, dead fish, petroleum,
> Worse than castoreum of mink or weasels,
> Saliva dripping from warm microphones,
> Agony of crucifixion on barstools.
>
> ("The Longing")

These lines do more than convey the living death of modern existence, they reveal the poet's feeling of disaffection from his true or spiritual nature. The soul withers in this climate, sickens on its fare; the effects are manifested outwardly in speech, gestures, looks. This "agony of crucifixion" calls for resurrection, and the poet asks "How to transcend this sensual emptiness?" Dreams will not suffice; actuality surrounds him everywhere in images of industrial urban landscape, dead and locked in itself; as a result, "the spirit fails to move forward, / . . . shrinks into a half-life, less than itself. . . ." Yet, in Part Two, the value of this "wretchedness" appears perhaps as cleansing preparatory to another

---

[4] Some of my remarks parallel those of Hugh Staples, whose "The Rose in the Sea-Wind: A Reading of Theodore Roethke's 'North American Sequence,'" *American Literature*, XXXVI (May, 1964), 189-203, I had not read at the time of this writing.

dream, large "enough to breathe in," which we see in the
striking images of the next lines shifting from dark to a
light whose strange flare beckons the poet. Both the image
of the rose—with all its traditional symbolic weight—and
the light—a source of grace and revelation in many recorded mystical experiences—announce a transcendent reality.
The stanza's concluding lines imply an accompanying spiritual renewal and potency ("bud" and "worm"). Another
short stanza ending this section shows the pattern of death
and rebirth which is the spirit's destiny if it chooses the
route to mystical communion. This pattern is further predicted in the image of the waning moon, the close of the lunar
cycle which, we know, merely precedes the beginning of a
new moon that will wax to the full:[5]

> What dream's enough to breathe in? A dark dream.
> The rose exceeds, the rose exceeds us all.
> Who'd think the moon could pare itself so thin?
> A great flame rises from the sunless sea;
> The light cries out, and I am there to hear—
> I'd be beyond; I'd be beyond the moon,
> Bare as a bud, and naked as a worm.
>
> To this extent I'm a stalk.
>   —How free; how all alone.
> Out of these nothings
>   —All beginnings come.

The absolute character of Roethke's quest is demonstrated by his desire to "be beyond the moon," that is, beyond
the recurrence of spiritual death and rebirth; this wish is
intensified as the poems proceed and may put us in mind of
Plotinus' memorable expression of the search for Divine

[5] For a discussion of lunar cycles, see Mircea Eliade, *The Sacred and
the Profane*, tr. Willard Trask (New York: Harcourt, Brace, 1959), pp.
155-59.

union, "the flight of the alone to the Alone." But while the
call to that union seems clearly uttered above, the realization is not so simple; and we will not be surprised, then, to
find that the third part of the poem returns to a middle
ground of recollection and meditation. The poet is no longer
vexed by the horrors of the poem's start, but neither is he
being swept up on waves of holy rapture to a beatific vision;
the journey has only begun. The long variable lines of this
section move with the currents of the poet's mind as he
awaits the impulse to spiritual movement which usually arrives without activity of the will, its origins located in that

> agency outside me.
> Unprayed-for,
> And final.
>   ("What Can I Tell My Bones?")

(Very often, as we might expect, the impulse is symbolized
naturalistically, normally by two of the four elements, air
and water, in the forms of wind and flowing waters or rivers.) Without this impulse, the spirit remains resident at the
center of the self, though not necessarily in a state of depression or emptiness; sometimes it engages in a period of
collecting itself, setting out its aims, calmly and beautifully
affirming the deep ties between human life and the natural
world that are such a remarkable feature of Roethke's poetry.

"Meditation at Oyster River" gets under way, as the title
suggests, in a specific place and sustains a familiar mood of
passive observation. The poet watches carefully "the first
tide ripples, moving"; his activity is minimal, his attention
directed at the spirit within to catch the first signs of an
awakening. The second section is a brief meditation provoked
by the spiritual inactivity of the first:

> The self persists like a dying star,
> In sleep, afraid. Death's face rises afresh,
> Among the shy beasts, the deer at the salt-lick,
> The does with the sloped shoulders loping across
>   the highway,
> The young snake, poised in green leaves, waiting
>   for its fly,
> The hummingbird, whirring from quince-blossom to
>   morning-glory—
> With these I would be.

A wish to discard the self, or at least to purify it to essentials, seems obvious here. In the first image Roethke exhibits the difficulty, for the self stays on as a residue in the same way that stars many light years away are still visible on earth long after they have actually been extinguished. The fear of losing oneself also clings; human nature and living creatures are further reminders of mortality, but this remembrance is changed into something more positive by identification of the poet with these creatures and, in the next stanza, with "the waves" and "the tongues of water" presaging spiritual movement. The longed-for dispersal of self into the beloved realms of nature is also integral to the course of mystical experience.

Memory takes command in the poem's third section, calls up river scenes from childhood that correspond with the present condition of the poet's inner life. Thus the exploding of the ice-blocked Tittebawasee River, so that "the whole river begins to move forward," is analogous to his own spiritual advance. In the dusky evening he sees the light of a new day breaking, feels at one with creation, and gives himself up to the "will" and direction of the water on whose surface the spirit will skim. In the last lines the moon reappears, inaugurating a new cycle.

"Journey to the Interior" acknowledges in its opening

"the long journey out of the self" and, like "The Far Field,"
supplies examples of it which end in frustration. Roethke
uses automobile trips through a variety of landscapes as
outward counterparts of the expedition to the center of the
self, that is, to the spirit. Much of the poem—and in this it
is very near to "The Long Waters" and "The Far Field" as
well as to preceding pieces in the sequence—is devoted to
rich geographical detail; here things are viewed from the
window of a passing car: small towns, bridges, animals, and
birds; elsewhere they are the things contemplated at the
water's edge by river or lake, or those others seen "at the
field's end, in the corner missed by the mower." Roethke
keeps us conscious during the entire sequence that his trav-
els are basically interior, and so the by now familiar pattern
of spiritual elation and depression, motion and relaxation, is
never obscured: "I rise and fall, and time folds / Into a
long moment. . . ." The self is now in what Miss Underhill
would call the "Way of Becoming" and receives from time
to time in the sequence the vision which accompanies a state
of heightened meditation. The last section of "Journey to
the Interior" presents the images visible to the poet in this
elevated condition, and the experience comes again, somewhat less sharply, at the finish of "The Long Waters"; assuming a more reflective cast, it closes "The Far Field" with
thoughts of the plan of human existence; "The Rose" folds
such experiences into the comprehensive image of that
flower, causing us to think of some of its other appearances,
in Dante, in Eliot and Yeats.

Each of the poems in the "North American Sequence" is
occupied with the spiritual journey but also with details of
place, through or from which moments of vision occur; and
so there is in every poem a substantial portion of magnificent descriptive writing, important in its links with the
inner life but delightful and evocative in itself. All this

is evident in "The Rose," toward which the other poems have
been leading. Place is insisted upon in the poet's position
"where sea and fresh water meet." When the busy life of
birds slackens and silence falls, he proceeds out of himself
"Into the darkening currents. . . ." Section Two enlarges
this exodus by a kind of epic simile of sea voyage and the
continuous "motion" of spiritual quest, but then turns to the
stable, unmoving yet surpassing image of the rose, rooted in
our world though extending beyond it. Stillness and movement, the journey and its goal, are contained in these lines:

> But this rose, this rose in the sea-wind,
> Stays,
> Stays in its true place,
> Flowering out of the dark,
> Widening at high noon, face upward,
> A single wild rose, struggling out of the white
>   embrace of the morning-glory. . . .

But again memory draws him back to childhood, to the familiar greenhouse of Roethke's early work, filled with roses:
". . . how those flowerheads seemed to flow toward me, to
beckon me, only a child, out of myself." Just so, the mystical rose of his mature experience attracts him to itself.

A long passage in Section Three catalogues a multitude of
things in the American landscape, specifically elements of
"sound and silence," but also whatever arrests the eye. The
rose image returns at the end and is pictured as a source of
nourishment to the thirsting spirit (see the kindred "flower
of all water, above and below me, the never receding, /
Moving, unmoving in a parched land" of "Journey to the
Interior") that will bring about the birth of a new self from
the old in the poet: Roethke introduces bird and flower images to suggest the freedom and transcendence of this
change, which may permit him to taste eternity and yet not

leave the world as we commonly know it. A balance between earthly and superior reality is implied in the ultimate stanza in the alternation of stone and light, sound and silence, self and sea-wind (the latter a vehicle of spiritual impulse). Roethke nears "the Unitive Life," to borrow from Evelyn Underhill another time, a life symbolically represented by the unchanging rose, whose shape and petals might also remind us in a more Jungian fashion of individuation and self-fulfillment in the mandala figure:

> Near this rose, in this grove of sun-parched, wind-
>   warped madronas,
> Among the half-dead trees, I came upon the true ease
>   of myself,
> As if another man appeared out of the depths of my
>   being,
> And I stood outside myself,
> Beyond becoming and perishing,
> A something wholly other,
> As if I swayed out on the wildest wave alive,
> And yet was still.
> And I rejoiced in being what I was:
> In the lilac change, the white reptilian calm,
> In the bird beyond the bough, the single one
> With all the air to greet him as he flies,
> The dolphin rising from the darkening waves;
>
> And in this rose, this rose in the sea-wind,
> Rooted in stone, keeping the whole of light,
> Gathering to itself sound and silence—
> Mine and the sea-wind's.

Among the other lyrics and love poems of *The Far Field* which come between "North American Sequence" and "Sequence, Sometimes Metaphysical," there is a slightly longer piece called "The Abyss," composed in the manner of "Meditations of an Old Woman" and much more tense and vertig-

inous than the poems we have just discussed. It opens on a
nervous interior colloquy:

> Is the stair here?
> Where's the stair?
> "The stair's right there,
> But it goes nowhere."
>
> And the abyss? the abyss?
> "The abyss you can't miss:
> It's right where you are—
> A step down the stair."

We are close to the "edge" here, that precarious border in
Roethke's poems between ecstasy and the void. In spite of
the calm and reconciliation at the end of "The Rose," he
has merely "been spoken to variously / But heard little" and
now lapses into a state not unlike the one which began "The
Longing." As in the second poem of "The Dying Man"
cycle, death approaches, "a sly surly attendant," but finally
departs, leaving the poet possessed of unpleasant images of
himself as a crawling caterpillar, a mole "winding through
earth, / A night-fishing otter." This part of the poem dis-
closes a reverse-motion of the spiritual life, a fall away from
vision; this experience of the abyss is that of a subjective
hell, or as it is spoken of a few lines later, "A flash into the
burning heart of the abominable."

In Section Four of "The Abyss" Roethke's statements become even more explicitly religious. His beginning rhetorical
questions again press him toward a supernatural goal:

> How can I dream except beyond this life?
> Can I outleap the sea—
> The edge of all the land, the final sea?

We find, too, the flowing waters of the Way of Becoming,
and then two stanzas about the poet's "knowing" and "not-

knowing" with regard to this spiritual process in which he is so completely absorbed. "Not-knowing" is related to the un-bidden spiritual impulse bringing him to visionary knowl-edge; reason gives no answers about this generating force: "We come to something without knowing why," Roethke says in "The Manifestation." But an attitude of religious reverence unmistakably marks the last stanza:

> The shade speaks slowly:
> "Adore and draw near.
> Who knows this—
> Knows all."

This attitude is carried into the final section, where the poet reveals his pleasure at communion with the Divine and at his release from the "heaviness" of spirit which tormented him before.

"North American Sequence" concludes under the symbol of the rose, but the lyrics of "Sequence, Sometimes Meta-physical" finish with the possibly more comprehensive, and certainly more energetic, image of a cosmic dance. The poems of this second sequence are, because of their formal manner, condensed in the presentation of experience; they bring their material to sudden, lively focus and seem to in-crease the range and depth of Roethke's mystical percep-tions by striking inward steadily with little recourse to external affairs. Unrelieved by descriptive writing, the atmos-phere is highly charged and passionate. Roethke goes past the achievements of the previous sequence in approximating the instant of naked revelation.

"In a Dark Time" was the subject of a brilliant symposi-um by John Crowe Ransom, Babette Deutsch, Stanley Kun-itz, and Roethke himself,[6] but I must venture to discuss the

---

[6] "The Poet and His Critics," ed. Anthony Ostroff, *New World Writing*, XIX (1961), 189-219.

poem because of its primary importance in the sequence. The poem is clearly about a moment of mystical illumination, but it also deals with the peripheral experiences, including spiritual unrest and agony, which precede and surround such a moment. Roethke plays on the word "dark" throughout the poem: the world of appearances darkens to physical sight, permitting a second or inner sight to take over; there is the dark of spiritual ignorance and of purgation to be endured; then we know, too, that there is a long tradition of mystical imagery in which the blazing light of God appears to our limited, impure human vision as an enveloping darkness. In the "echoing wood," recalling Dante, the poet meets, as he has said, "my double, my Other, usually tied to me, my reminder that I am going to die,"[7] and advances into a personal darkness, which he characterizes as a "Hades." There he loses dignity and control in the midst of familiar nature: "A lord of nature weeping to a tree." The humiliation and self-abasement of weeping are replaced by suggestions of madness as an exalted defiance of "circumstance" and of despair while the self descends into the inferno of its undoing. A "place among the rocks" at which the poet next arrives is a decisive threshold in the journey, since it must be either a dead-end, and thus a real place of death, or a point where movement alters direction and goes upward, out of these depths: "That place among the rocks —is it a cave, / Or winding path? The edge is what I have." Fortunately, it is the "winding path," reminiscent of the path spirits traverse between the natural and supernatural worlds in Yeats's "Byzantium." These two worlds seem to mix in Roethke's vision as well: things are seen as transparent and symbolic, unveiling their higher significances. The last lines of stanza three indicate that a "death of the self" or self-purgation is necessary in order to see "All natu-

[7] *Ibid.*, p. 215.

ral shapes blazing unnatural light" (by "unnatural"
Roethke surely means "supernatural").

The final stanza powerfully sets forth the urgency of the
soul's desire for a Divine union:

> Dark, dark my light, and darker my desire.
> My soul, like some heat-maddened summer fly,
> Keeps buzzing at the sill. Which I is *I?*
> A fallen man, I climb out of my fear.
> The mind enters itself, and God the mind,
> And one is One, free in the tearing wind.

Again Roethke emphasizes the darkness of his vision; the
greater darkness of his "desire," I suppose, connotes his aim
to win an even more intimate meeting with God. The soul,
freed momentarily of the attachments of self, seeks a total
release from earthly reality but is restrained, in part at
least, by the poet's double nature which emerges once more
in the question, "Which I is *I?*" These dilemmas are tempo-
rarily healed in the Divine embrace of the closing lines,
where the mind regains unity, is seized and assimilated by
God, and so learns a kind of absolute freedom. The "tearing
wind" is obviously the breath of spiritual force we have
often noticed; at this instant it is, understandably, at its
strongest.

Roethke said of this poem that it was "the first of a sequence, part of a hunt, a drive toward God . . . ,"[8] and we
can expect, therefore, that the other pieces will be involved
with such mystical experience or with interpretations of it.
These concerns hold the sequence together, as do recurrent
words and images. "In Evening Air" offers a respite from
the intense strain of Divine vision, allowing the poet to ru-
minate on that vision, its demands upon the self, and to
reassert his artistic vocation: "I'll make a broken music, or

[8] *Ibid.,* p. 214.

I'll die." Most important, he can still utter his love for creation and his prayerful request for transcendence at the same time. The rose image is used again to blend natural and supernatural spheres of being:

> Ye littles, lie more close!
> Make me, O Lord, a last, a simple thing
> Time cannot overwhelm.
> Once I transcended time:
> A bud broke to a rose,
> And I rose from a last diminishing.

Roethke begins "The Sequel" as a poem of self-questioning, queries his motives, the character of his experience; but soon he sees "a body dancing in the wind" which distracts his attention. This is a figure of more than one meaning: first, his guide, his Beatrice, who appears frequently in love poems and other earlier lyrics; second, the *anima* or soul, which is a female principle in the male (see "The Restored" in this sequence, where it has a poem to itself). The figure heralds another spiritual awakening and engages the poet in a dance of universal celebration that continues into "The Restored" and reaches a climax in "Once More, the Round." Corresponding rather closely to the dance and the female figure is the image of "An old wind-tattered butterfly" that "pulsed its wings upon the dusty ground" in "stretchings of the spirit" at the start of "The Motion"; the conclusion of this poem is another realization of possibility which aids the poet on his trying way: "O, motion O, our chance is still to be!"

Located near the middle, the poem "Infirmity" summarizes various themes worked through the entire sequence, much as "The Lost Son" does in the "Praise to the End" sequence. "Infirmity" explores at first Roethke's wish to retain his individual identity and yet "to be something else."

Pride, fear, and self-love prevent him from abandoning himself wholly to the spirit: this is one aspect of infirmity in the poem. The second stanza, concerned with his physical nature, describes another sort of infirmity: the slow death of the body which will force the poet out of himself, into the realm of the spirit, by killing him. A little wryly, he thinks Christ must be pleased with this inevitability:

> Sweet Christ, rejoice in my infirmity;
> There's little left I care to call my own.
> Today they drained the fluid from a knee
> And pumped a shoulder full of cortisone;
> Thus I conform to my divinity
> By dying inward, like an aging tree.

Here the tree refers explicitly to the poet's life, and the description of that life's gradual collapse extends through the next stanza, where "a pure extreme of light / Breaks" on the poet as his "meager flesh breaks down" and he becomes "son and father of [his] only death." The increase of spiritual life, then, seems exactly proportionate to the decrease of physical powers, and—"The soul delights in that extremity." Roethke muses on this terrible and frightening transformation of himself in stanza four; there "the deep eye" of second sight "sees the shining on the stone," an altered version of the dance we have noted, and also the play of Divine light. "The eternal seeks, and finds, the temporal," he writes; and we feel something of the enormous pressure of that spiritual impulse which leads the poet where it will. He is brought one more time, through the symbolism of the lunar cycle, to a death of the self and a rebirth "beyond the reach of wind and fire." In the subsequent stanza he states again his abiding love for the creatures of the natural world and recognizes that he has not lost everything he valued as his own, for, as he says, "My soul is still my soul, and still the Son, / And knowing this, I am not yet undone." The soul is, in other words, born of the body's decrepitude and, at last, its death, but it keeps a personal quality, the signs of the individual's life and loves:

> Things without hands take hands: there is no choice,—
> Eternity's not easily come by.
> When opposites come suddenly in place,
> I teach my eyes to hear, my ears to see
> How body from spirit slowly does unwind
> Until we are pure spirit at the end.

Roethke gives voice in these final lines to the transforming process he knows himself to be undergoing. His means of apprehending experience change to conform with the radically different zones of reality into which he is being thrust, and so the ordinary sensory perception is replaced by synesthesia (reputedly common in mystical experience). Indeed, we might say that the moment of mystical union in "In a Dark Time" is a conditioning for this last journey in death of which Roethke speaks in the concluding line above; such a journey, of course, lies beyond the province of poetry, except as it is glimpsed in vision.

"The Decision," "The Marrow," "I Waited," and "The Tree, the Bird" all concentrate in strong fashion on episodes in the Way of Becoming: periods of waiting, discontent; the agony involved in choosing to pursue this Way; the acts of sacrifice and self-annihilation required to progress toward God ("I bleed my bones, their marrow to bestow / Upon that God who knows what I would know"); the tension of inner division; and those hard-won but rewarding visions that pierce through time:

> The present falls, the present falls away;
> How pure the motion of the rising day,
> The white sea widening on a farther shore.

> The bird, the beating bird, extending wings—.
> Thus I endure this last pure stretch of joy,
> The dire dimension of a final thing.
> ("The Tree, the Bird")

Roethke intends, I believe, by "dire" not something evil or fatal, in a pejorative sense, but rather something overpowering that puts aside whatever has preceded it.

Even though the spiritual journey Roethke has embarked upon and carried through, in spite of considerable pain and uncertainty, to a peak of mystical knowledge may appear to us as anything but a pleasurable venture, he can still persuade us in "The Right Thing" that he is "the happy man."[9] This poem is primarily about that spiritual impulse, often seen in the form of wind and water, to which the poet submits himself throughout these late poems. Determinacy of a spiritual nature, or perhaps we should call it Divine necessity, brings Roethke to a transcending joy; he "takes to himself what mystery he can,"

> And, praising change as the slow night comes on,
> Wills what he would, surrendering his will
> Till mystery is no more: No more he can.
> The right thing happens to the happy man.

The final poem of the sequence maintains the same elated feelings. It begins with a question—"What's greater, Pebble or Pond?"—about the worth of the isolated spirit as it is drawn into the heart of Absolute Reality, and repeats the desire for knowledge of "The Unknown." In this initial stanza we discover also the image of the "true self" running toward "a Hill" (which recalls Dante's "purgatorial hill" to which Roethke refers in "Four for Sir John Davies") or,

---

[9] "I count myself among the happy poets," Roethke wrote earlier in "Open Letter," in *Mid-Century American Poets,* ed. John Ciardi (New York: Twayne, 1950), p. 70.

ultimately, toward God. That self is the real "I" of the two confusing the poet in "In a Dark Time," and it is a new self born of the spirit, purged of dross and yet keeping its attachment to creation. So the poet celebrates this spiritual birth by joining in a dance of cosmic proportions with all creatures and things, and with Blake, whose vision ("the Eye altering all"), like Roethke's, can find God living in everything and everything living in God; all are in One and One is in all:

> Now I adore my life
> With the Bird, the abiding Leaf,
> With the Fish, the questing Snail,
> And the Eye altering all;
> And I dance with William Blake
> For love, for Love's sake;
>
> And everything comes to One,
> As we dance on, dance on, dance on.

Roethke's search for God ends poetically in that inclusive and joyous representation of a Divine unity. Theodore Roethke, it seems to me, is one of our great American poets; and in "North American Sequence" and "Sequence, Sometimes Metaphysical" he has left us not only some of his finest work but a number of the most astonishing mystical poems in the language.

DENIS DONOGHUE

Roethke's Broken Music

HERE IS A POEM CALLED "SNAKE" IN WHICH THEO-
dore Roethke describes a young snake turning and
drawing away; and then he says:

> I felt my slow blood warm.
> I longed to be that thing,
> The pure, sensuous form.
>
> And I may be, some time.

To aspire to a condition of purity higher than any available
in the human world is a common urge. Poets who want to
burn with a hard, gem-like flame often give this condition as
a pure, sensuous form, nothing if not itself and nothing beyond itself. But it is strange, at first sight, that Roethke
gives his parable in the image of a snake, because snakes
tend to figure in his poems as emblems of the sinister. In
"Where Knock Is Open Wide" one of the prayerful moments reads: "I'll be a bite. You be a wink. / Sing the snake
to sleep." In "I Need, I Need" the phrase "snake-eyes" is
enough to send its owner packing. And there is this, in
"The Shape of the Fire": "Up over a viaduct I came, to the
snakes and sticks of another winter, / A two-legged dog

hunting a new horizon of howls." But this is at first sight, or at first thought; because Roethke, more than most poets, sought a sustaining order in the images of his chaos, and only those images would serve. If you offer a dove as answer to a snake, your answer is incomplete, an order not violent enough. Hence when the right time came, in "I'm Here," Roethke would find that a snake lifting its head is a fine sight, and a snail's music is a fine sound, and both are joys, credences of summer. As Roethke says in "The Longing": "The rose exceeds, the rose exceeds us all."

But he did not sentimentalize his chaos. He lived with it, and would gladly have rid himself of it if he could have done so without an even greater loss, the loss of verifiable life. When he thought of his own rage, for instance, he often saw it as mere destructiveness: in one of his early poems he said: "Rage warps my clearest cry / To witless agony." And he often resorted to invective, satire, pseudonymous ti-rades, to cleanse himself of rage and hatred. In one of those tirades he said, "Behold, I'm a heart set free, for I have taken my hatred and eaten it." But "Death Piece" shows that to be released from rage is to be—quite simply—dead. And the price is too high. This is one of the reasons why Roethke found the last years of W. B. Yeats so rewarding; because Yeats made so much of his rage, in the *Last Poems, The Death of Cuchulain,* and *Purgatory.* In one of his own apocalyptic poems, "The Lost Son," Roethke says, "I want the old rage, the lash of primordial milk," as if to recall Yeats's cry, "Grant me an old man's frenzy." And in "Old Lady's Winter Words" he says: "If I were a young man / I could roll in the dust of a fine rage . . . " and in "The Senten-tious Man": "Some rages save us. Did I rage too long? / The spirit knows the flesh it must consume." Hence Roethke's quest for the saving rage. Call it—for it is this— a rage for order. He was sometimes tempted to seal himself

against the rush of experience, and he reminds himself in
"The Adamant" that the big things, such as truth, are sealed
against thought; the true substance, the core, holds itself
inviolate. And yet man is exposed; exposes himself. And, in
a sense, rightly so. As Yeats says in the great "Dialogue of
Self and Soul,"

> I am content to live it all again
> And yet again, if it be life to pitch
> Into the frog-spawn of a blind man's ditch. . . .

In "The Pure Fury" Roethke says, "I live near the
abyss." What he means is the substance of his poetry. The
abyss is partly the frog-spawn of a blind man's ditch, partly
a ditch of his own contriving, partly the fate of being human
in a hard time, partly the poet's weather. As discreetly as
possible we can take it for granted, rehearsing it only to the
extent of linking it with the abyss in other artists. Better to
think of it as the heart of each man's darkness. In "Her Becoming" Roethke speaks of it, in one aspect:

> I know the cold fleshless kiss of contraries,
> The nerveless constriction of surfaces—
> Machines, machines, loveless, temporal;
> Mutilated souls in cold morgues of obligation.

And this becomes, in the "Fourth Meditation," "the dreary
dance of opposites." (But so far it is common enough.)

It is still common enough when Roethke presents it
through the ambiguities of body and soul. In "Epidermal
Macabre" Roethke, like Yeats in *The Tower,* wishes the
body away in favor of a spirit remorselessly sensual:

> And willingly would I dispense
> With false accouterments of sense,
> To sleep immodestly, a most
> Incarnadine and carnal ghost.

Or again, when the dance of opposites is less dreary, Roethke
accepts with good grace the unwinding of body from soul:

> When opposites come suddenly in place,
> I teach my eyes to hear, my ears to see
> How body from spirit slowly does unwind
> Until we are pure spirit at the end.
>
> ("Infirmity")

Sometimes the body is "gristle." In "Praise to the End!"
Roethke says, "Skin's the least of me," and in the "First
Meditation" it is the rind which "hates the life within."
(Yeats's "dying animal" is clearly visible.) But there were
other moments, as there were in Yeats. In "The Wraith" the
body casts a spell, the flesh makes the spirit "visible," and
in the "Fourth Meditation" "the husk lives on, ardent as a
seed."

Mostly in Roethke the body seems good in itself, a primal
energy. And when it is this, it features the most distinctive
connotations of the modern element: it is a good, but ill at
ease with other goods. Above all, it does not guarantee an
equable life in the natural world. More often than not, in
these poems, man lives with a hostile nature, and lives as
well as he can. In "I Need, I Need" intimations of waste,
privation, and insecurity lead to this:

> The ground cried my name:
> Good-bye for being wrong.
> Love helps the sun.
> But not enough.

"I can't marry the dirt" is an even stronger version, in
"Bring the Day," echoing Wallace Stevens' benign "mar-
riage of flesh and air" while attaching to it now, as coura-
geously as possible, the bare note, "A swan needs a pond";
or, more elaborately in another poem, "A wretch needs his

wretchedness." The aboriginal middle poems have similar
cries on every page: "These wings are from the wrong
nest"; "My sleep deceives me"; "Soothe me, great groans
of underneath"; "Rock me to sleep, the weather's wrong";
"Few objects praise the Lord."

These are some of Roethke's intimations of chaos; they
reach us as cries, laments, protests, intimations of loss. Most
of Roethke's later poems are attempts to cope with these intimations by becoming—in Stevens' sense—their connois-
seur. In "The Dance" Roethke speaks of a promise he has
made to "sing and whistle romping with the bears," and
whether we take these as animals or constellations, the
promise is the same and hard to keep. To bring it off at all
Roethke often plays in a child's garden, especially in poems
like "O Lull Me, Lull Me" where he can have everything he
wants by having it only in fancy. "Light fattens the rock,"
he sings, to prove that good children get treats. "When I say
things fond, I hear singing," he reports, and we take his
word for it; as we do again when we acknowledge, in a later
poem, that "the right thing happens to the happy man."
Perhaps it does. But when Roethke says "I breathe into a
a dream, / And the ground cries . . ." and again "I could say
hello to things; / I could talk to a snail;" we think that he
protests too much and we know that his need is great.

Roethke is never quite convincing in this note, or in the
heynonny note of his neo-Elizabethan pastiche. Even when
he dramatizes the situation in the "Meditations of an Old
Woman" the answers come too easily: in two stanzas he has
"the earth itself a tune" and this sounds like a poet's wish-
ful dreaming. Roethke may have wanted the kind of tone
which Stevens reached in his last poems, an autumnal calm
which retains the rigor and the feeling but banishes the fret-
ful note, the whine, the cry of pain. But Stevens earned this.
And Yeats earned it, too, in poems like "Beautiful Lofty

Things." Roethke claimed it without really earning it. Here is a stanza from "Her Becoming":

> Ask all the mice who caper in the straw—
> I am benign in my own company.
> A shape without a shade, or almost none,
> I hum in pure vibration, like a saw.
> The grandeur of a crazy one alone!—
> By swoops of bird, by leaps of fish, I live.
> My shadow steadies in a shifting stream;
> I live in air; the long light is my home;
> I dare caress the stones, the field my friend;
> A light wind rises: I become the wind.

And here is Stevens, a passage from "The Course of a Particular":

> The leaves cry. It is not a cry of divine attention,
> Nor the smoke-drift of puffed-out heroes, nor human cry.
> It is the cry of leaves that do not transcend themselves,
> In the absence of fantasia, without meaning more
> Than they are in the final finding of the air, in the thing
> Itself, until, at last, the cry concerns no one at all.

How can we compare these two passages except to say that Stevens speaks with the knowledge that there have been other days, other feelings, and the hope that there will be more of each, as various as before? Roethke speaks as if the old woman were now released from time and history and the obligations of each, released even from the memories which she has already invoked. There is too much fantasia in Roethke's lines, and this accounts for a certain slackness which fell upon him whenever he tried too hard to be serene. Stevens' poem is, in the full meaning of the word, mature; Roethke's is a little childish, second-childish. Stevens would affirm, when affirmation seemed just, but not before.

Roethke longed to affirm, and when the affirmation would not come he sometimes—now and again—dressed himself in affirmative robes.

But only now and again. At his best he is one of the most scrupulous of poets. In "Four for Sir John Davies," for instance, the harmony between nature and man which Davies figured—the orchestra, the dance, the music of the spheres; all this is brought to bear upon the poem, critically and never naïvely or sentimentally: the divinely orchestrated universe of Davies' poem is more than a point of reference but far less than an escape-route. For one thing, as Roethke says, "I need a place to sing, and dancing-room," and for another, there is no dancing-master; and, for a third, there isn't even at this stage a dancing partner. So he must do the best he can in his poverty. And if his blood leaps "with a wordless song," at least it leaps: "But what I learned there, dancing all alone, / Was not the joyless motion of a stone." But even when the partner comes and they dance their joy, Roethke does not claim that this makes everything sweet or that nature and man will thereafter smile at each other. In the farthest reach of joy he says: "We danced to shining; mocked before the black / And shapeless night that made no answer back." The sensual cry is what it is, and there are moments when it is or seems to be final, but man still lives in the element of antagonisms. In *Four Quartets* the "daun-synge"-scene from Sir Thomas Elyot testifies to modes of being, handsome but archaic; it answers no present problem. Nor does Sir John Davies, who plays a similar role in Roethke's sequence. And even before that, in "The Return," man in the element of antagonisms feels and behaves like an animal in his "self-infected lair," "With a stump of scraggy fang / Bared for a hunter's boot." And sometimes he turns upon himself, in rage.

When Roethke thinks of man in this way, he often pre-

sents him in images of useless flurry. He is clumsy, ungainly, an elephant in a pond. Roethke often thinks of him
as a bat; by day, quiet, cousin to the mouse; at night, crazy,
absurd, looping "in crazy figures." And when the human situation is extreme, Roethke thinks of man as a bat flying
deep into a narrowing tunnel. Far from being a big, wide
space, the world seems a darkening corridor. In "Bring the
Day!" Roethke says, "Everything's closer. Is this a cage?"
And if a shape cries from a cloud as it does in "The Exorcism," and calls to man's flesh, man is always somewhere
else, "down long corridors." (Corridors, cages, tunnels,
lairs: if these poems needed illustration, the painter is easily
named; Francis Bacon, keeper of caged souls.)

In "Four for Sir John Davies" the lovers, Roethke says,
"undid chaos to a curious sound," curious meaning careful
as well as strange and exploratory. In this world, to undo
chaos is always a curious struggle, sometimes thought of as
a release from constriction, a stretching in all directions, an
escape from the cage. In "What Can I Tell My Bones?"
Roethke says, "I recover my tenderness by long looking,"
and if tenderness is the proof of escape, long looking is one
of the means. In *King Lear* it is to see feelingly. In some of
Roethke's poems it is given as, quite simply, attention. In
"Her Becoming" Roethke speaks of a "jauntier principle
of order," but this is to dream. What he wants, in a world of
cages and corridors, is to escape to an order; an order of
which change and growth and decay are natural mutations
and therefore acceptable. In many of the later poems it will
be an order of religious feeling, for which the punning motto
is: "God, give me a near."

The first step, the first note toward a possible order, is to
relish what can be relished. Listening to "the sigh of what
is," one attends, knowing or at least believing that "all finite
things reveal infinitude." If things "flame into being," so

much the better. "Dare I blaze like a tree?," Roethke asks
at one point, like the flaming tree of Yeats's "Vacillation."
And again Roethke says, "What I love is near at hand, /
Always, in earth and air." This is fine, as far as it goes, but
it is strange that Roethke is more responsive to intimations
of being when they offer themselves in plants than in
people; and here, of course, he differs radically from Yeats.
In the first version of "Cuttings" he is exhilarated when
"the small cells bulge"; when cuttings sprout into a new
life; when bulbs hunt for light; when the vines in the forcing house pulse with the knocking pipes; when orchids draw
in the warm air; when beetles, newts, and lice creep and
wriggle. In "Slug" he rejoices in his kinship with bats, wea-
sels, and worms. In "A Walk in Late Summer" being "delights in being, and in time." In the same poem Roethke delights in the "midnight eyes" of small things, and in several
poems he relishes what Christopher Smart in *Jubilate Agno*
calls "the language of flowers." Everywhere in Roethke
there is consolation in the rudimentary when it is what it is,
without fantasia. It is a good day when the spiders sail into
summer. But Roethke is slow to give the same credences to
man. Plants may be transplanted, and this is good, but what
is exhilarating reproduction in insects and flowers is mere
duplication in people. Girls in college are "duplicate gray
standard faces"; in the same poem there is talk of "endless
duplication of lives and objects." Man as a social being is
assimilated to the machine; the good life is lived by plants.
In the bacterial poems weeds are featured as circumstance,
the rush of things, often alien but often sustaining. "Weeds,
weeds, how I love you," Roethke says in "The Shape of the
Fire." In the "First Meditation," "On love's worst ugly
day, / The weeds hiss at the edge of the field, . . ." In
"What Can I Tell My Bones?," "Weeds turn toward the
wind weed-skeletons," presumably because "the dead love

the unborn." But in "Praise to the End!," when the water is low and romping days are over, "the weeds exceed me."

There are two ways of taking this, and Roethke gives us both. Normally, we invoke the rudimentary to criticize the complex: the lower organism rebukes the higher for falling short of itself, as body rebukes the arrogance of vaunting mind or spirit. This works on the assumption that what is simple is more "natural" than what is complex, and that lower organisms have the merit of such simplicity. Or, alternatively, one can imply that the most exalted objects of our human desire are already possessed, in silence and grace, by the lower organisms. Roethke has this. In "The Advice," for instance, he says:

> A learned heathen told me this:
> Dwell in pure mind and Mind alone;
> What you brought back from the Abyss,
> The Slug was taught beneath his Stone.

—presumably because the slug had a teacher, perhaps the dancing-master who has retired from the human romp. Roethke does not commit the sentimentality of implying, however, that all is sweetness and light in the bacterial world, and generally he avoids pushing his vegetal analogies too far. In his strongest poems the bacterial is featured as a return to fundamentals, a syntax of short phrases to represent the radical breaking-up which may lead to a new synthesis. In grammatical terms; we have broken the spine of our syntax by loading it with our own fetiches. So we must begin again as if we were learning a new language, speaking in short rudimentary phrases. Or, alternatively: we learn in simple words and phrases, hoping that eventually we may reach the light of valid sentences. In this spirit Roethke says, in a late poem, "God bless the roots!—Body and soul are one!" The roots, the sensory facts, are beneath or beyond doubt: in

"The Longing" Roethke says, "I would believe my pain:
and the eye quiet on the growing rose." Learning a new language in this way, we must divest ourselves, at this first
stage, of all claims to coherence, synthesis, or unity: this is
the secular equivalent of the "way of purgation" in *Four
Quartets,* and it serves a corresponding purpose, because
here too humility is endless. If our humility is sufficient; if
we attend to the roots, to beginnings; we may even be re-
warded with a vision in which beginning and end are one. As
in the poem "In Evening Air":

> Ye littles, lie more close!
> Make me, O Lord, a last, a simple thing
> Time cannot overwhelm.
> Once I transcended time:
> A bud broke to a rose,
> And I rose from a last diminishing.

We can see how this goes in the first stanzas of "Where
Knock Is Open Wide":

> A kitten can
> Bite with his feet;
> Papa and Mamma
> Have more teeth.

We can take this as pure notation; the primitive vision linking things which to the complex adult eye seem incommen-
surate. But the adult eye is "wrong" and it must go to
school again if it is ever to say, "I recover my tenderness by
long looking." Roethke's lines are "intuitions of sensibility,"
the ground of our beseeching; acts of the mind at the very
first stage, long before idea, generalization, or concept. And
this is the only way to innocence. Or so the poem suggests.
Then the second stanza:

> Sit and play
> Under the rocker
> Until the cows
> All have puppies.

Here the aimlessness of the kitten stands for the innocence of game and apprehension. The play is nonchalant and it conquers time by the ease of its reception. Time is measured by the laws of growth and fruition, not by the clock. In this sense it is proper to say, as Roethke does in the next stanza,

> His ears haven't time.
> Sing me a sleep-song, please.
> A real hurt is soft.

In Christopher Smart's "A Song to David"—which is the source of the title of the present poem[1]—stanza 77 includes the lines:

> And in the seat to faith assigned
> Where ask is have, where seek is find,
> Where knock is open wide.

The cat's ears haven't time because they don't ask for it; if time is for men the destructive element, that is their funeral, and mostly their suicide. "Sing me a sleep-song, please" is a prayer to be released from time. "A real hurt is soft" is an attempt to render human pain as pure description, to eliminate self-pity. And the appropriate gloss is the second stanza of "The Lost Son," "Fished in an old wound, / The soft pond of repose, . . ."—to remind us that the primitive vision is at once harsh and antiseptic. (Roethke himself sometimes forgot this.) Hence these intuitions of rudimentary sensibility are exercises, akin to spiritual exercises, all the better if they are caustic, purgative, penitential. The exercises are

[1] I owe this to James G. Southworth.

never finished, because this is the way things are, but once they are well begun the soul can proceed; the energy released is the rage for a sustaining order.

The search for order begins easily enough in Roethke: sometimes, as we have seen, it begins in celebration, relishing what is there to relish. Or again it may begin by sounding a warning note. The early poem "To My Sister" is a rush of admonition designed for survival and prudence. "Defer the vice of flesh," he tells her, but on the other hand, "Keep faith with present joys." Later, Roethke would seek and find value in intimations of change and growth. And then in love, normally sexual love. Many of the love poems are beautiful in an Elizabethan way, which is one of the best ways, and whether their delicacy is entirely Roethke's own or partly his way of acknowledging the delicacy of Sir Thomas Wyatt is neither here nor there. Some of the love poems are among Roethke's finest achievement: I would choose "The Renewal," "I Knew a Woman," "The Sensualists," "The Swan," "She," and "The Voice." Or, merely because it is shorter, this one, "Memory":

> In the slow world of dream,
> We breathe in unison.
> The outside dies within,
> And she knows all I am.
>
> She turns, as if to go,
> Half-bird, half-animal.
> The wind dies on the hill.
> Love's all. Love's all I know.
>
> A doe drinks by a stream,
> A doe and its fawn.
> When I follow after them,
> The grass changes to stone.

Love was clearly a principle of order, in Roethke's poems, but it never established itself as a relation beyond the bedroom. It never became dialogue, or *caritas*. Outside the bedroom Roethke became his own theme, the center of a universe deemed to exist largely because it had such a center. This does not mean that the entire universe was mere grist to his mill; he is not one of the predatory poets. But on the other hand he does not revel in the sheer humanity of the world. Indeed, his universe is distinctly underpopulated. Even Aunt Tilly entered it only when she died, thereby inciting an elegy. This is not to question Roethke's "sincerity": poems are written for many reasons, one of which is the presence of poetic forms inviting attention. But to indicate the nature of Roethke's achievement it is necessary to mark the areas of his deepest response and to point to those areas which he acknowledged more sluggishly, if at all. I have already implied that he responded to the human modes of being only when a specific human relation touched him and he grasped it: he did not have that utter assent to other people, other lives, which marks the best poetry of William Carlos Williams or Richard Eberhart, the feeling that human life is just as miraculous as the growth of an orchid or the "excess" of a rose. Indeed, one might speculate along these lines; that Roethke's response to his father and mother and, in the love poems, to his wife was so vivid that it engrossed all other responses in the human world; it set up a monopoly.

Even when he acknowledged a natural order of things, Roethke invariably spoke of it as if it did not necessarily include the human order; or as if its inclusion of that order were beside the point. The natural order of things included moss growing on rock, the transplanting of flowers, the cycle of mist, cloud, and rain, the tension of nest and grave. It might even include what he calls, rather generally, "the wild

disordered language of the natural heart." But the question
of the distinctively human modes of life was always problematic. In Roethke's poems human life is endorsed when it
manages to survive a storm; as in "Big Wind," where the
greenhouse—Roethke's symbol for "the whole of life"—
rides the storm and sails into the calm morning. There is
also the old florist, standing all night watering the roses;
and the single surviving tulip with its head swaggering over
the dead blooms. And then Otto.

To survive; to live through the weeds; in Roethke's world
you do this by taking appropriate security measures. Property is a good bet. In "Where Knock Is Open Wide" there
is a passage which reads:

> That was before. I fell! I fell!
> The worm has moved away.
> My tears are tired.
>
> Nowhere is out. I saw the cold.
> Went to visit the wind. Where the birds die.
> How high is have?

The part we need is the last line, "How high is have?" In
several poems Roethke will pray for a close relation to God,
and this will rate as security, but in the meantime even
property in a material sense will help. And because he lived
in our own society and sought order from the images of his
chaos, security and property meant money. In "The Lost
Son," for instance, there is this:

> Good-bye, good-bye, old stones, the time-order is going,
> I have married my hands to perpetual agitation,
> I run, I run to the whistle of money.
>
> Money money money
> Water water water

—and even if he wrote two or three poems to make fun of this, the fact remains; property and the fear of dispossession, money and the lack of it, were vivid terms in his human image. Property was money in one's purse, more reliable than most things.

More reliable than reason, for instance. In his search for a viable and live order, Roethke used his mind for all it was worth, but he would not vote for reason. He did not believe that you could pit the rational powers against the weeds of circumstance and hope to win. When he spoke of reason, it was invariably Stevens' "Reason's click-clack," a mechanical affair. In one poem Roethke says, "Reason? That dreary shed, that hutch for grubby schoolboys!" Indeed, reason normally appears in his poems, at least officially, as a constriction. Commenting on his poem "In a Dark Time," Roethke said that it was an attempt "to break through the barriers of rational experience."[2] The self, the daily world, reason, meant bondage: to come close to God you had to break through; these things were never the medium of one's encounter with God, always obstacles in its way. For such encounters you had to transcend reason; if you managed it, you touched that greater thing which is the "reason in madness" of *King Lear*. The good man takes the risk of darkness. If reason's click-clack is useless there remains in man a primitive striving toward the light. Nature, seldom a friend to man, at least offers him a few saving analogies; one being that of darkness and light. Much of this is given in the last stanzas of "Unfold! Unfold!":

> Sing, sing, you symbols! All simple creatures,
> All small shapes, willow-shy,
> In the obscure haze, sing!

[2] "The Poet and His Critics," ed. Anthony Ostroff, *New World Writing*, XIX (1961).

A light song comes from the leaves.
A slow sigh says yes. And light sighs;
A low voice, summer-sad.
Is it you, cold father? Father,
For whom the minnows sang?

> A house for wisdom; a field for revelation.
> Speak to the stones, and the stars answer.
> At first the visible obscures:
> Go where light is.

To go where light is: the object is self-possession; sometimes featured as a relation to the world:

> I lose and find myself in the long water;
> I am gathered together once more;
> I embrace the world.
>   ("The Long Waters")

To be one's own man; to come upon "the true ease of myself"; to possess oneself so fluently as to say, "Being, not
doing, is my first joy": these are definitive joys, when "the
light cries out, and I am there to hear—." If it requires "the
blast of dynamite" to effect such movements, well and good;
at any cost Roethke must reach the finality in which, as he
says in "Meditation at Oyster River," "the flesh takes on
the pure poise of the spirit." (This is his version of Yeats's
"Unity of Being.") Hence he admires the tendrils which do
not need eyes to seek, the furred caterpillar that crawls
down a string; anything that causes movement, gives release, breaks up constriction. In the natural world there is
growth, the flow of water, the straining of buds toward the
light. And in the poet's craft these move in harmony with
the vivid cadence, fluency, Yeats's "tact of words," the leaping rhythm.

For the rest, Roethke's symbolism is common enough.

The life-enhancing images are rain, rivers, flowers, seed, grain, birds, fish, veins. The danger signals are wind, storm, darkness, drought, shadow. And the great event is growth, in full light. "The Shape of the Fire" ends:

To have the whole air!—
The light, the full sun
Coming down on the flowerheads,
The tendrils turning slowly,
A slow snail-lifting, liquescent;
To be by the rose
Rising slowly out of its bed,
Still as a child in its first loneliness;
To see cyclamen veins become clearer in early sunlight,
And mist lifting out of the brown cattails;
To stare into the after-light, the glitter left on the lake's surface,
When the sun has fallen behind a wooded island;
To follow the drops sliding from a lifted oar,
Held up, while the rower breathes, and the small boat drifts
    quietly shoreward;
To know that light falls and fills, often without our knowing,
As an opaque vase fills to the brim from a quick pouring,
Fills and trembles at the edge yet does not flow over,
Still holding and feeding the stem of the contained flower.

The flower, contained, securely held in a vase filled with water and light: with this image we are close to the core of Roethke's poetry, where all the analogies run together. The only missing element is what he often called "song," the ultimate in communication, and for that we need another poem, another occasion. One of his last poems, a love poem, ends:

We met to leave again
The time we broke from time;
A cold air brought its rain,
The singing of a stem.

> She sang a final song;
> Light listened when she sang.
>   ("Light Listened")

If light listens; if light attends upon a human event; then
the event is final. Kenneth Burke has pointed out that
Roethke tends to link things, whenever there is a choice, by
means of a word in the general vocabulary of communication. We need only add this; that when the relation is as
close as a relation can be, the participants "sing," and there
is singing everywhere; singing and listening. "The light
cries out, and I am there to hear."

Pushed to their conclusion, or followed to their source,
these analogies would run straight to the idea of God; or
rather to the image of God. And taking such stock in the
symbolism of creation and light, Roethke could hardly have
avoided this dimension. Nor did he. One of his greatest
poems is called "The Marrow":

> The wind from off the sea says nothing new.
> The mist above me sings with its small flies.
> From a burnt pine the sharp speech of a crow
> Tells me my drinking breeds a will to die.
> What's the worst portion in this mortal life?
> A pensive mistress, and a yelping wife.
>
> One white face shimmers brighter than the sun
> When contemplation dazzles all I see;
> One look too close can take my soul away.
> Brooding on God, I may become a man.
> Pain wanders through my bones like a lost fire;
> What burns me now? Desire, desire, desire.
>
> Godhead above my God, are you there still?
> To sleep is all my life. In sleep's half-death,
> My body alters, altering the soul
> That once could melt the dark with its small breath.

> Lord, hear me out, and hear me out this day:
> From me to Thee's a long and terrible way.
>
> I was flung back from suffering and love
> When light divided on a storm-tossed tree.
> Yea, I have slain my will, and still I live;
> I would be near; I shut my eyes to see;
> I bleed my bones, their marrow to bestow
> Upon that God who knows what I would know.

The first stanza is all alienation—from nature and man and the self. The second is preparation for prayer, a relation with God as the light of light, source of the sun. The third is the prayer itself to the Ground of All Beseeching. In the fourth and last stanza the loss of selfhood is associated with the break-up of light on a storm-tossed tree, the emaciation of the human will; and then the last gesture, the voiding of the self, restitution, atonement. (A characteristic sequence in late Roethke.)

From the poems I have quoted it might seem that Roethke was concerned with only one thing: himself. And this is true. But in his case it does not mean what it usually does. I do not mean that he is thrilled by his own emotions, or that he spends much time in front of his mirror. The saving grace, in Roethke as in Whitman, is the assumption that he is a representative instance, no more if no less. When he searches for value and meaning, he assumes that this is interesting insofar as it is representative and not at all interesting when it ceases to be so. This is the source of Roethke's delicacy, as of Whitman's. When he says, in "I Need, I Need," "The Trouble is with No and Yes"; or when he says, in "The Pure Fury," "Great Boehme rooted all in Yes and No"; he advances this choice as a universal predicament rather than a proof of his own tender conscience. Again, in "The Waking" and other poems of similar intent,

when he says "I learn by going where I have to go," he is
not claiming this as a uniquely sensitive perception; the line
points to areas of feeling that are important because universal. And when he says, "Light takes the Tree; but who can
tell us how?," the question is given with notable modesty,
although indeed Roethke could have staked a higher claim
for it since it is the basis of several of his own religious
poems. The motto for this delicacy in Roethke is a line from
"The Sententious Man": "Each one's himself, yet each
one's everyone." And there is the "Fourth Meditation" to
prove that Roethke was never really in danger of solipsism.

With these qualifications, then, it is permissible to say
that he was his own theme and to consider what this means
in the poems. With this point in mind, however; that Whitman's equations were not available to Roethke. Roethke
was not content to think of the self as the sum of its contents, even if he had Yeats to tell him that a mind is as rich
as the images it contains. He would try to accumulate property, but only because he thought of property as a protec-
tive dike; behind the dike, one could live. But he never
thought of this as having anything to do with the "nature"
of the self; the self was problematic, but not a problem in
addition. In one of his last and most beautiful poems, "In a
Dark Time," he said,

> A man goes far to find out what he is—
> Death of the self in a long, tearless night,
> All natural shapes blazing unnatural light.
>
> Dark, dark my light, and darker my desire.
> My soul, like some heat-maddened summer fly,
> Keeps buzzing at the sill. Which I is *I?*

That is still the question. In the early poems Roethke held
to the common Romantic idea of "the opposing self," the

self defined by its grappling with the weeds of circumstance; hence, as Hopkins said, "Long Live the Weeds."
Much later, Roethke was to consider this more strictly, notably in a poem like "The Exorcism," where he asks in a be-
guiling parenthesis: "(Father of flowers, who / Dares face
the thing he is?)." And this question is joined to several
bacterial images of man partaking uneasily of several
worlds. In "Weed Puller" man is down in a fetor of weeds
"Crawling on all fours, / Alive, in a slippery grave." Many
of the middle poems feature a declared loss of self, often
given as division, absence. In "Where Knock Is Open Wide"
Roethke says

> I'm somebody else now.
> Don't tell my hands.
> Have I come to always? Not yet.
> One father is enough.
>
> Maybe God has a house.
> But not here.

There is a similar feeling in "Sensibility! O La!," and in
" 'The Shimmer of Evil' " perhaps the most explicit of all
versions is, quite simply, "And I was only I"—which leads
almost predictably but nonetheless beautifully to "There
was no light; there was no light at all." The later poems
tend to reflect upon the nature of the self by listing its demands; behind the love poems there is the assertion that
"we live beyond / Our outer skin," even when the body
sways to music. And much of this feeling culminates in the
lovely "Fourth Meditation," which begins with many intuitions of sensibility and goes on to this:

But a time comes when the vague life of the mouth no longer
   suffices;
The dead make more impossible demands from their silence;

The soul stands, lonely in its choice,
Waiting, itself a slow thing,
In the changing body.

> The river moves, wrinkled by midges,
> A light wind stirs in the pine needles.
> The shape of a lark rises from a stone;
> But there is no song.

This is a later version of the predicament, loss of self, which cries through the middle poems. In "The Lost Son" there is

> Snail, snail, glister me forward,
> Bird, soft-sigh me home.
> Worm, be with me.
> This is my hard time.

—and a few lines later, "Voice, come out of the silence. / Say something." But there is no song in that "kingdom of bang and blab." In Roethke's poems song is proof that infinity clings to the finite. In "Old Lady's Winter Words" he says, "My dust longs for the invisible." What he wants is given in phrase, image, and rhythm; ". . . the gradual embrace / of lichen around stones"; "Deep roots"; and, quite directly, "Where is the knowledge that / Could bring me to my God?" The only knowledge is reason in madness.

Theodore Roethke was a slow starter in poetry. He survived and grew and developed without attaching himself to schools or groups. He was never a boy wonder; he was never fashionable as the Beat poets were fashionable; most of the currents of easy feeling left him untouched, unmoved. He never set up shop as a Left Wing poet or a Right Wing poet or a Catholic poet or a New England poet or a Southern poet or a Californian poet; he never claimed privilege in any region of feeling. This was probably as good for his poetry as it was bad for his fame. He made his way by slow movements, nudgings of growth, like his own plants and flowers. But he grew, and his poems got better all the time; so much so, that his last poems were his greatest achievements, marvelously rich and humane.

Along the way, he was helped by friends, often poets like Louise Bogan and Marianne Moore; but this is another story, not mine to tell. But he was helped also by other writers, earlier poets, and some of this story can be told. Or at least we may suggest a few footnotes to the main text. Clearly, he was a careful, scrupulous poet. There are lines and phrases here and there which show that he was prone to infection, picking up things from lesser poets, like Dylan Thomas, and keeping them beyond the call of prudence. But the poets who really engaged him were those who offered him a challenge, a mode of feeling, perhaps, which he himself might not possess; or, possessed without knowing that he did. The Elizabethan song-poets, and especially John Donne, challenged him in this way, and Roethke's love poems reflect not only their own feeling but the strenuous competition of the Elizabethan masters. And then there were poets like Davies and Smart who disclosed certain modes of feeling and belief which were not so deeply a personal challenge but a measure of the time in which we live. And there were the great modern masters whom he could hardly have avoided hearing. He learned a lot from T. S. Eliot; mainly, I think, how to be expressive while holding most of his ammunition in reserve. And this often comes through the verse as a cadence, as in this passage from "I'm Here":

> At the stream's edge, trailing a vague finger;
> Flesh-awkward, half-alive,
> Fearful of high places, in love with horses;

> In love with stuffs, silks,
> Rubbing my nose in the wool of blankets;
> Bemused; pleased to be;
> Mindful of cries,
> The meaningful whisper,
> The wren, the catbird.

The rhetoric of the short phrase, at once giving and taking; T. S. Eliot is a great master in these discriminations—think of this passage in "East Coker":

> In the middle, not only in the middle of the way
> But all the way, in a dark wood, in a bramble,
> On the edge of a grimpen, where is no secure foothold,
> And menaced by monsters, fancy lights,
> Risking enchantment.

Other cadences Roethke got from other poets; from Hopkins, notably, especially from "The Wreck of the Deutschland," which Roethke uses in the poem about the greenhouse in a storm, "Big Wind":

> But she rode it out,
> That old rose-house,
> She hove into the teeth of it,
> The core and pith of that ugly storm. . . .

From Joyce, Roethke learned one kind of language for the primitive, the rudimentary, the aboriginal; especially the Joyce of the *Portrait of the Artist as a Young Man,* bearing hard on the first chapter; and *Finnegans Wake* showed him one way of dealing with the unconscious. And there is Wallace Stevens: Roethke disapproved of Stevens' procedures, in argumentative theory, but in fact he learned some fundamental lessons from Stevens. When he says, "I prefer the still joy," he is Stevens' pupil, conning a lesson he could well have done without. And I think he found in Stevens a justification, if not an incitement, of his own propensity for the "pure moment." In one of his later poems he says, "O to be delivered from the rational into the realm of pure song," and if pure song is pure expression or pure communication it is also close to Stevens' "hum of thoughts evaded in the mind." Stevens seems to me to be behind those poems in which Roethke longs for essence, for an essential "purity," or finds it in a still moment. A passage like this, for instance, from the "First Meditation":

> There are still times, morning and evening:
> The cerulean, high in the elm,
> Thin and insistent as a cicada,
> And the far phoebe, singing,
> The long plaintive notes floating down,
> Drifting through leaves, oak and maple,
> Or the whippoorwill, along the smoky ridges,
> A single bird calling and calling;
> A fume reminds me, drifting across wet gravel;
> A cold wind comes over stones;
> A flame, intense, visible,
> Plays over the dry pods,
> Runs fitfully along the stubble,
> Moves over the field,
> Without burning.
>> In such times, lacking a god,
>> I am still happy.

And Stevens is behind those poems in which Roethke presents the "single man" who contains everything:

> His spirit moves like monumental wind
> That gentles on a sunny blue plateau.
> He is the end of things, the final man.
>> ("The Far Field")

When Whitman comes into the later poems, such as "Journey to the Interior," he shows Roethke how to deal with

natural forms without hurting them, so that "the spirit of
wrath becomes the spirit of blessing"; or how to give one
thing after another without lining them up in Symbolist ri-
valry, so that he can say "Beautiful my desire, and the place
of my desire"; or how to preserve one's own integrity even
when beset by "the terrible hunger for objects." (But Whitman was a late consultant to Roethke.) Much earlier, and to
the end of his poetic life, he attended upon Yeats's poems
and contracted debts handsomely acknowledged in the "In
Memoriam" and again in "The Dance." To Roethke—or so
it seems from the poems—Yeats stood for the imperious
note, concentration, magnificent rhetoric clashing against
the bare notation, the dramatic play of self and soul:

> What's madness but nobility of soul
> At odds with circumstance? The day's on fire!
> I know the purity of pure despair,
> My shadow pinned against a sweating wall.
> That place among the rocks—is it a cave,
> Or winding path? The edge is what I have.
>   ("In a Dark Time")

It peters out somewhat: Yeats would not have praised the
last line. But the rest is very much in Yeats's shadow, particularly the Yeats of "Coole Park and Ballylee, 1931." The
dramatic occasion; the landscape, moralized with a large
showing; the poet, finding correspondences and emblems in
herons, wrens, swans; nature with her tragic buskin on:
these are the Yeatsian gestures. And—to take them a little
further—Roethke knows that if he proposes to learn a high
rhetoric he must do it in earnest. So he begins with the mag-
isterially rhetorical question; then the short declaration, not
yet intimate, "The day's on fire!" And only then the despair;
and even now it is given as knowledge rather than Romantic exposure; so that even the shadow, the other self, is

given as an object of contemplation before the poet acknowledges the feeling as his own in "a sweating wall."

One of the odd things in this list of relationships, however, is that it is quite possible to think of Roethke as one of
the best modern poets without troubling about the fact that
he was, after all, an American poet. When reading Stevens
or Robert Frost or William Carlos Williams or Robert Lowell we are constantly aware that we are reading American
poets; but this is not an insistent element in Roethke. Indeed
it is quite clear that he bears no special relation to either of
the dominant traditions in American poetry—New England
and the South. Temperamentally, he is not too far away from
such writers as Hawthorne, Melville, or James; like them, in
his quite different way, he was concerned with the wounded
conscience, the private hazard. But while it is obviously
proper in some sense to relate the poems of Robert Lowell to
this tradition, it has little bearing on Roethke's work. And the
tradition of the South can be ruled out. This suggests that
the discussion of American literature in terms of these two
traditions may by now have lost much of its force. To think
of the New England tradition as scholastic, autocratic, and
logical; and the Southern tradition as humanistic, Cicero-
nian, grammatical, and rhetorical;[3] this is fine as far as it
goes, but its relevance clearly fades in regard to poets like
Roethke. This may well be the point to emphasize; that
Roethke and many of the poets of his generation took their
food wherever they could find it. Yeats could well be more
useful to them than, say, Hawthorne because they saw their
problems as being human, universal, in the first instance,
and American problems only by application and inference.
Roethke committed himself to his own life, such as it was.
He thought of it as a human event of some representative

[3] Cf. H. M. McLuhan, "Poe's Tradition," *Sewanee Review*, LII (1944),
31f.

interest. And he set himself to work toward lucidity and
order without turning himself into a case study entitled
"The Still Complex Fate of Being an American." This is one
aspect of Roethke's delicacy. Contemporary American
poets, for the most part, are not going his way; they insist
upon their complex fate and would not live without it. But
Roethke's way of being an American is an eminently re-
spectable way, and part of his achievement is that he makes
it available to others.

"The Far Field" is a distinguished example of this delicacy. It has four unequal sections. The first is a dream of
journeys, journeys without maps, featuring imprisonment,
attenuation of being, the self "flying like a bat deep into a
narrowing tunnel" until there is nothing but darkness. It is
life in a minor key, diminished thirds of being. The second
stanza translates these into major terms, images of force,
aggression, suffering, death, dead rats eaten by rain and
ground beetles. But the poet, meditating upon these images,
thinks of other images, of life, movement, freedom, everything he means by "song." And these natural configurations
lead to thoughts of life as cycle, evolution and return, prolif-
erations of being, the whole process of life which the poet
calls "infinity"; what Wallace Stevens in "The Bouquet"
calls

> the infinite of the actual perceived,
> A freedom revealed, a realization touched,
> The real made more acute by an unreal.

In the third section the poet feels a corresponding change in
himself, a moving forward, a quickening, and as he commits
himself to earth and air he says, "I have come to a still, but
not a deep center." Naturally, it feels like a loss, another
diminution of being, even if the sense of life-ordained
process is strong. And this feeling leads straight into the
fourth and last section:

> The lost self changes,
> Turning toward the sea,
> A sea-shape turning around,—
> An old man with his feet before the fire,
> In robes of green, in garments of adieu.
>
> A man faced with his own immensity
> Wakes all the waves, all their loose wandering fire.
> The murmur of the absolute, the why
> Of being born fails on his naked ears.
> His spirit moves like monumental wind
> That gentles on a sunny blue plateau.
> He is the end of things, the final man.
>
> All finite things reveal infinitude:
> The mountain with its singular bright shade
> Like the blue shine on freshly frozen snow,
> The after-light upon ice-burdened pines;
> Odor of basswood on a mountain-slope,
> A scent beloved of bees;
> Silence of water above a sunken tree:
> The pure serene of memory in one man,—
> A ripple widening from a single stone
> Winding around the waters of the world.

"The end of things, the final man"; or, as Stevens put it in "The Auroras of Autumn":

> There is nothing until in a single man contained,
> Nothing until this named thing nameless is
> And is destroyed. He opens the door of his house
> On flames. The scholar of one candle sees
> An Arctic effulgence flaring on the frame
> Of everything he is. And he feels afraid.

The difference is that Stevens identifies the man with his imagination, and his imagination with his vision; and insists upon doing so. And the imagination feeds upon as much reality as it can "see" and values only that: what it can't see won't hurt or help it. The scholar has only this one candle. Roethke's man is not a scholar at all, or if he is, he is an amateur, perhaps a mere teacher. His imagination is partly his memory; which offers hospitality to sights, sounds, and smells: and partly his conscience: and partly his feeling for modes of being which he cannot command, directions which he cannot chart. Hence his poems are the cries of their occasions; but rarely cries of triumph. This is what makes his later poems the noble things they are; stretchings of the spirit without fantasia or panache. "Which is the way?" they ask, and if they include God in their reply they do so with due deference, knowing that one can be "too glib about eternal things," too much "an intimate of air and all its songs."

Another way of putting it: the poems, especially the middle poems, are cries of their occasions, sudden, isolated cries; the later poems turn cries into prayers, praying for a world-order, a possible world-harmony of which the cries are part, like voices in polyphony. The self in exposure is monotone; a sustaining society is polyphony; God is the Great Composer. The poet's ideal is the part-song, music for several instruments, what the Elizabethans called "broken music." In "In Evening Air" Roethke says, "I'll make a broken music, or I'll die." In such poems as "The Marrow" and "In a Dark Time" he made a broken music at once personal and—in Stevens' sense—noble. And then, alas, he died.

ROY HARVEY PEARCE

Theodore Roethke
The Power of Sympathy

For Robert Estrich
"What you survived I shall believe . . ."

T THE END OF WALLACE STEVENS' "THE NOBLE RIDER
and the Sounds of Words" there is a passage which
may serve as prolegomenon to the poetics of our
recent past:

The mind has added nothing to human nature. It is a violence from
within that protects us from a violence without. It is the imagination pressing back against the pressure of reality. It seems, in the
last analysis, to have something to do with our self-preservation; and
that, no doubt, is why the expression of it, the sound of its words,
helps us live our lives.

Using the passage, one can trace some of the relationships
between the work of the great elder modernists (Stevens
and his generation) and of the poets who come immediately
after. The work of the former defines the poet's vocation according to an extreme choice, whereby he may attend either
to the violence without or to the violence within. Only thus

may he master the ways of violence with sensibility and learning; only thus transform violence into process, that process of art which form charts for us. Stevens himself is pre-eminently the poet of the opposing self; Eliot is the poet of the opposing other. And the poets of the generations after Eliot and Stevens, necessarily mindful of their elders' ways, have as necessarily accepted their elders' definition of the poet's vocation: how, through the exercise of his craft, to contain violence, whatever its origin and end, so as to make it a source of power.

At bottom, then, the issue for the poet is the issue for modern man in all his capacities and institutions: power. The commonplace is nonetheless true for being a commonplace. The conditions of modern life have at once created and tapped sources of a force so great that it must inevitably issue as violence. For the poet what threatens is an entropy of the sensibility as it manifests itself in language. And yet he has access to the sensibility only through language. If language—either as he knows it within or as he knows it without—runs mad with the terror of that to which it refers, the poet must yet live with it, live through it. He needs power; so he must put himself vitally in touch with violence. The touch is everything. He knows that violence cannot be attenuated, much less done away with. But it can be transformed into power, so then to bring into consonance the life of the spirit and the life of society—the self alone and the self as other coordinate with other, perhaps higher, selves.

Theodore Roethke's achievement takes on its special meaning from the fact that he single-mindedly searched out violence in its very sources and strove mightily to find such modes of order as would transform it into power—the power of sympathy, the means to reach across the gulf which separates the sources of the violence within from those of the violence without. The paradigm for his poetry is this: violence transformed into power through order. The structure and technique of the poems enact the transformation, and would create a kind of spiritual exercise whereby the reader might learn the lessons of the poet's life.

For in Roethke's work the poet's life is always insistently there. Sometimes it is too much so, to be sure, and the exercise leads to no end but wonderment about the poet as private person. In such cases, the process limits rather than transforms, leading to curiosity rather than self-knowledge. Roethke himself seems to have known this. And as he put his poems into volumes, he tried consistently to eliminate from his collections verses in which the requisite transformative factor, for whatever reason, is absent. "Feud," for example, put into *Open House* but not subsequently reprinted, begins:

> Corruption reaps the young; you dread
> The menace of ancestral eyes;
> Recoiling from the serpent head
> Of fate, you blubber in surprise.
>
> Exhausted fathers thinned the blood,
> You curse the legacy of pain;
> Darling of an infected brood,
> You feel disaster climb the vein.

The manner is not really Roethke's, we may decide, but, say, Allen Tate's. Still, what is lacking in (not wrong with) the poem—when viewed in the light of the poems as Roethke selected and ordered them in *Words for the Wind* —is a means of involving the reader directly in the lucubrations of the speaker. The reader is that "you," and finds himself accused, but as the later Roethke might have decided, not sufficiently tutored into an understanding of the accusation. "Feud" ends:

> You meditate upon the nerves,
> Inflame with hate. This ancient feud
> Is seldom won. The spirit starves
> Until the dead have been subdued.

The violence remains without, to be stoically resisted, perhaps conquered—in any case, not understood. The violence within—which empowers the resisting—is controlled and focused by rhetoric, and someone else's at that. "Feud" is a considerable poem, and persuasive. The later Roethke—I daresay the authentic Roethke—wanted to do more than persuade. The authentic Roethke, as he sought to define himself, is not he who, in language on loan, would persuade the living that they must subdue the dead. For a poem like "Feud" rather commemorates than celebrates, rather neutralizes violence than transforms it, rather shuns power than seeks it. The authentic Roethke came to be the celebrant of the transformation of violence into power.

It is this growing sense of his own vocation, I think, which led Roethke not to put into his volumes his poems about life in mental hospitals—for example, "Lines Upon Leaving" (1937), "Meditation in Hydrotherapy" (1937), and "Advice to One Committed" (1960). The last named begins:

> Swift's servant beat him; now they use
> The current flowing from a fuse,
> Or put you on a softer diet;
> Your teeth fall out—but you'll be quiet;
> Forget you ever were someone—
> You'll get ten minutes in the sun.

There is a fine Swiftian quality to such poems. But they are too neat. They are objectively rather than subjectively personal, and (when viewed in the light of what Roethke came to demand of his verse) just will not do. "The Return"

(1946), however, Roethke did put into *The Lost Son* and
kept in *The Waking* and *Words for the Wind:*

> I circled on leather paws
> In the darkening corridor,
> Crouched closer to the floor,
> Then bristled like a dog.
>
> As I turned for a backward look,
> The muscles in one thigh
> Sagged like a frightened lip.
>
> A cold key let me in
> That self-infected lair;
> And I lay down with my life,
> With the rags and rotting clothes,
> With a stump of scraggy fang
> Bared for a hunter's boot.

The importance of specific occasion and locale here is diminished exactly as the significance of the experience is increased; such details as we are given are internalized into a
sequence of metaphors which urge us to participate in the
poem and to use it as a means of defining our own return to
the mental hospitals—if such are meant here—which we
perforce make out of our lives. The violence of the controlling metaphor—marked by "circled," "crouched," "bris-
tled," "sagged," "self-infected," and "bared"—such violence is countered, then transformed, by that "And I lay
down with my life." For it is the power of lying down—but
still *with* one's life—which finally dominates and teaches us
to defy the hunter's boot. The difference between "Advice to
One Committed" and "The Return" is the difference between death-in-life and life-in-death.

   For violence leads to death—alternatively to the death of
the self at the hands of the other, or the death of the other

at the hands of the self. This Roethke saw and felt and understood more deeply and with greater intelligence than any poet of our time. He sought to find a means of refusing the either/or option which his culture offered him. The design of *Words for the Wind* and *The Far Field* manifests that search. In choosing earlier poems to reprint, in adding new poems, in grouping them, he mapped out his quest so as to make it his readers'. He rejected not only such "autobiographical" poems as I have cited but a number of wonderfully funny poems attacking persons who threatened—not so much himself as what he increasingly stood for. Also, he rejected a number of poems bitingly observant of modern urban life. One guesses that he was overreacting to his own aggressiveness, as though it too were a form of violence which threatened. (Although he had some of this cake and ate it too: in the pieces he published under the pseudonym "Winterset Rothberg.") He would—as he depicted the growth of the poet's mind—observe violence, and carefully annotate it; and he would turn it only upon himself. Thus he discovered the nature and working of violence, studied the transformative role of order, and found the power to become a poet.

The first poem in *Words for the Wind* is the title poem from *Open House*. Preserving it, and the four which immediately follow, Roethke preserves himself as public spokesman. "Open House" is, in contrast to the bulk of the poems, somewhat "rhetorical." Its general mode is like that of "Feud"—persuasive. Moreover, it rather declares than develops:

> My secrets cry aloud.
> I have no need for tongue.
> My heart keeps open house,
> My doors are widely swung.

> An epic of the eyes
> My love, with no disguise.

So many figurations—each to be accepted or declined separately, but each leading to the closing lines:

> I stop the lying mouth:
> Rage warps my clearest cry
> To witless agony.

Roethke was to reverse the order described here: to transform agony, by virtue of the transformation no longer witless, into a clearest cry, hence to transcend rage. Doing so, he was to move beyond rhetoric into the actual processes of consciousness.

He had to begin at the beginning—with primitive things. For him, understanding the natural order of primitive things came to be a means to and model for understanding all in the natural order, himself included, which is beyond the primitive. What the natural order contains, and therefore manifests, is growth—what seems to be violence but is not, for it is directed toward an end, as power must be if it is truly to be power. And in the rest of the poems kept from *Open House* the poet is caught in the excitement of his own crashing-through to the edge of just this insight. After a "Mid-Country Blow," he writes: "When I looked at the altered scene, my eye was undeceived, / But my ear still kept the sound of the sea like a shell." "The Heron" is described with the greatest exactitude as he moves; and then "A single ripple starts from where he stood." Roethke would be following, tracing out, that single ripple the rest of his life. But in these poems it is enough—more would be at this stage too much—that he see it at only the outset; that in "No Bird" he define one dead as being beyond the "breeze above her head" and the "grasses [which] whitely stir"; that (reversing a figure from Marvell) he proclaim "Long live the weeds that

overwhelm / My narrow vegetable realm!" Wonderment is
enough—the wonderment of the lovely "Vernal Sentiment":
"I rejoice in the spring, as though no spring ever had been."
Intermixed as it is with such poems, the declarative "Open
House," like others of its kind in the *Words for the Wind* sequence after which it is named, gains a vitality which is not
its own when it is taken separately. "Night Journey," which
concludes the sequence, details a cross-country train trip,
with its myriad revelations:

> Bridges of iron lace,
> A suddenness of trees,
> A lap of mountain mist. . . .

Because he can see in such things the kind of vitality and
growth revealed to him in the more telling poems of the sequence, Roethke is justified at the end in returning to his
declarative mode: "I stay up half the night / To see the
land I love."

Inevitably (so the design of *Words for the Wind* indicates), Roethke's journey was—as he said in so many words
in the title of a late poem—into the interior. First the interi-
or was that of the natural order, and then his own, to the
degree that he was part of the natural order. The design of
Words for the Wind, as it emerges at this stage, is the design of another *Song of Myself*, or another *Prelude*—as in
later poems Roethke himself makes quite clear, perhaps
having discovered only later that the design, worked out ret-
rospectively, had a certain necessity of its own. At this point,
having discovered the vitality, violence, and power of the
natural order, he was obliged to understand it. He had,
then, to move away from the rather safe and simplistic
forms of *Open House* to forms adequate to the understanding he would achieve: a structure of verse which would ar-

ticulate the essential facts and qualities of its primitive realm and, at the same time, be expressive of the act of articulation itself. Roethke's was to be a lover's battle with his world; victory would result only if it were fought to a draw. The risks, in the context of modernist verse, were great: to dare the heresy of the pathetic fallacy and that of imitative form. And there were failures, to be sure. One takes them as the price paid for successes. And, because one can be doubly retrospective, one looks ahead to the poems beyond those from *The Lost Son,* which make up the second sequence in *Words for the Wind.*

At this stage, Roethke is surest of himself in his greenhouse poems. He seems wholly to comprehend the natural order and those, including himself, who are close to it. At first glance, the effect of the poems is to impute human qualities to the natural world; at second glance, once the poems have had their way, the effect is to discover those qualities in great and complex detail. There is then established a new order of understanding: that such qualities, precisely as they are human, are derived from the natural order. A kind of underground dialectic is everywhere at work, an argument generated by the organization and movement of the poems.

> Sticks-in-a-drowse droop over sugary loam,
> Their intricate stem-fur dries;
> But still the delicate slips keep coaxing up water;
> The small cells bulge; . . .
>
> ("Cuttings")

"Sticks-in-a-drowse" and "coaxing" register human qualities; but "intricate" and "delicate" (such commonplace descriptive words they are) work to qualify and classify the implied anthropomorphic claim, and to establish a more-than-analogical relationship between perceiver and things perceived. The act of perception, when it is expressed, is one with the growth, the vital principle, of the things perceived. Thus, in "Cuttings, *later*" the poet can say that he knows exactly what is going on here, knows it unmediated:

> This urge, wrestle, resurrection of dry sticks,
> Cut stems struggling to put down feet,
> What saint strained so much,
> Rose on such lopped limbs to a new life?
>
> I can hear, underground, that sucking and sobbing,
> In my veins, in my bones I feel it,—
> The small waters seeping upward,
> The tight grains parting at last.
> When sprouts break out,
> Slippery as fish,
> I quail, lean to beginnings, sheath-wet.

The natural world is not the emblem of self-knowledge and self-realization, but the source and occasion of their being. One sees, one hears, one knows, and one is. Or at least, one begins to be.

The poet discovers this in others—the subjects of "Old Florist" and "Frau Bauman, Frau Schmidt, and Frau Schwartze," for example. But most of all, he discovers it in himself—as a "Weed Puller"

> ... down in that fetor of weeds,
> Crawling on all fours,
> Alive, in a slippery grave;

and in "Moss Gathering," when

> ... afterwards I always felt mean, jogging back over the logging road,
> As if I had broken the natural order of things in that swampland;
> Disturbed some rhythm, old and of vast importance,
> By pulling off flesh from the living planet;
> As if I had committed, against the whole scheme of life,
>   a desecration.

The "natural order of things" and the "scheme of life,"
then, must be his central subject. The papa who, in all his
power, waltzes so surely; the boy, at sixteen, itching with
the lust of good smells in the pickle factory; the mother,
dwelling in "That fine fuming stink of particular kettles"—
these he must understand because they are closest to the
"natural order of things" and the "scheme of life." Yet their
world, with all its unself-conscious spontaneity, is lost to
him. And, as I have pointed out, he must begin at the beginning, studying "The Minimal," the "lives on a leaf," which
are "Cleaning and caressing, / Creeping and healing."

He concludes the poems kept from *The Lost Son* with
another one in his declarative mode. By now, however, that
mode has been qualified by and accommodated to the mode
which is dominant in *The Lost Son*.

> Dark water, underground,
> Beneath the rock and clay,
> Beneath the roots of trees,
> Moved into common day,
> Rose from a mossy mound
> In mist that sun could seize.
>
> The fine rain coiled in a cloud
> Turned by revolving air
> Far from that colder source
> Where elements cohere
> Dense in the central stone.
> The air grew loose and loud.
>
> Then, with diminished force,
> The full rain fell straight down,
> Tunneled with lapsing sound
> Under even the rock-shut ground,
> Under a river's source,
> Under primeval stone.
> ("The Cycle")

Surely, we are to recall the end of *The Waste Land* here. And Roethke is initiating a grand dialogue with one of his modernist masters. He too would Give, Sympathize, Control —come to know the sources of power, in order at once to make proper obeisance to them and to share in them. The rain that comes to save his land, however, comes from underground, and returns there, only again and again to move through, in the title of the poem, "The Cycle." The poet, in short, must discover his own cycle, his own underground, his own relationship to the source under the primeval stone.

In *Words for the Wind* Roethke puts into the section called "Praise to the End" not only poems from the volume of that name but the closing sequence of *The Lost Son.* This sequence does indeed belong where he places it; for, like the sequence kept from *Praise to the End!*, it most fully manifests the violence of Roethke's journey into the interior— beyond childhood with its order (of a sort), beyond the order of the natural world, to the swirling, threatening, inchoate sources of his very being. The Wordsworthian title of the section, and the *Prelude* passage from which the title comes, are helpful, in that they sum up and categorize Roethke's effort here:

> How strange, that all
> The terrors, pains, and early miseries,
> Regrets, vexations, lassitudes interfused
> Within my mind, should e'er have borne a part,
> And that a needful part, in making up
> The calm existence that is mine when I
> Am worthy of myself! Praise to the end!

Writing a kind of apologia for those poems which comprise the "Praise to the End" section, Roethke explained:

. . . the method is cyclic. I believe that to go forward as a spiritual man it is necessary first to go back. Any history of the psyche (or allegorical journey) is bound to be a succession of experiences, similar yet dissimilar. There is a perpetual slipping-back, then a going-forward; but there is *some* "progress." Are not some experiences so powerful and so profound (I am not speaking of the merely compulsive) that they repeat themselves, thrust themselves upon us, again and again, with variation and change, each time bringing us closer to our own most particular (and thus most universal) reality? We go, as Yeats said, from exhaustion to exhaustion. To begin from the depths and come out—that is difficult; for few know where the depths are or can recognize them; or, if they do, are afraid.[1]

We need guidance like this, if only to prepare ourselves for the exhaustion which is our proper due.

The style of these poems is regressive, but out of the regression there comes a certain progression, a deepening of one's sense of the fact, the factuality, of consciousness itself. The poems seem to anticipate the effort to comprehend them, and to defy it; yet the thrust of defiance is itself a thrust *toward* the reader and on his behalf—so, paradoxically, a crucial factor in his mode of comprehension. The language is most often that of the earliest stages of childhood, thus only barely language; it is charged with the force of the primary process of consciousness and so threatens always to disintegrate. Roethke is closest to the entropy of sensibility here. That infantile amnesia which psychoanalysis has discovered for us is broken through, or almost.[2]

---

[1] *Mid-Century American Poetry,* ed. John Ciardi (New York, 1950), p. 69.

[2] I must state flatly that the poems are supersaturated with language out of Freud and Jung, or their myriad exegetes. See, however, Carolyn Kizer, "Poetry of the Fifties in America," in *International Literary Annual,* ed. John Wain (London, 1958), p. 84: "I should probably say here that Roethke has not read Joyce or Jung; and that, in 1952, after all his long poems exploring a child's history of consciousness had appeared, he was discovered in a Morris chair by a friend, with a copy of Freud's *Basic Writings* on one arm, his book *Praise to the End!* on the other, and his notebook in his lap, checking references, and chortling to himself, 'I was right! I was right!'" One can only suppose that the friend mistook Winterset Rothberg for Theodore Roethke.

And yet, as Roethke claims, these are "traditional" poems. The tradition is that deepest in the sensibility of individual men; it is a composite of their childhood experiences, experiences so deeply lived through as to seem the experience of the world from which, as children, they could not yet properly differentiate themselves. Coming at this point in the sequence of Roethke's poems, they establish the conditions under which it is possible to see how, in autobiographical fact, a man is part of the natural order in general and of his own natural order in particular. The literary source of the language is appropriately traditional too, as Roethke noted: "German and English folk literature, particularly Mother Goose; Elizabethan and Jacobean drama, especially the songs and rants; the Bible; Blake and Traherne; Dürer."[3] What the poems demand of a reader is a willing suspension of adult consciousness, and yet a firm and controlled sense of oneself in the act of willing that suspension—which is, indeed, in recording the growth of his poet's mind, what they must have demanded of Roethke.

In a sense, they are not poems but rather pre-poems; so that the reader, working through them, must bring his own capacities as protopoet most actively to bear on them. In effect, the reader *completes* them. One can hardly talk about these poems, or in terms of them. One can only try to talk through them—which perhaps is a way, a way we too much neglect, of learning, all over again, to talk. Thus the first section of the first poem in the six-poem sequence which begins "Praise to the End," "Where Knock Is Open Wide":

> A kitten can
> Bite with his feet;
> Papa and Mamma
> Have more teeth.

[3] Ciardi (ed.), *Mid-Century American Poetry*, p. 71.

> Sit and play
> Under the rocker
> Until the cows
> All have puppies.

His ears haven't time.
Sing me a sleep-song, please.
A real hurt is soft.

> Once upon a tree
> I came across a time,
> It wasn't even as
> A ghoulie in a dream.

> There was a mooly man
> Who had a rubber hat
> And funnier than that,—
> He kept it in a can.

> What's the time, papa-seed?
> Everything has been twice.
> My father is a fish.

Let us say that this is an entrance-into-the-world poem. For the child, cause and effect are not "rationally" related—thus it is the knock, not the door, which opens wide on this experience; the kitten's scratches with his feet are in effect identical with teeth-bites; and if time is measured by gestation and birth, it is no matter that cows don't have puppies. When the father will not listen, it is his ears, not his larger self, that decline. And in the deepest world of once-upon, the distinction between time and place is of no significance. Papa generates, therefore must be seed, therefore has a sense of time. Like papa, like son; therefore everything has been twice. And further, in this world, papa is primeval, is therefore a fish, swimming through time. What intrudes it-

self everywhere is the adult world, which threatens the
world of the child, precisely as it promises so much to that
world. A real hurt is in fact a hurt, as the child's world is
threatened; but it is at the same time soft, as it is a hurt
from the adult world which promises so much.

We can read such verse only in this way. Even as in its
art Roethke's poem gets us to consent to the world it estab-
lishes, we report the news of that world back to the one in
which we actually live. We do the world of these verses
wrong if we translate it into a language appropriate to ours.
Rather we must incorporate it, incorporate its style of ap-
perception and knowing, into our own. Thus the way of exhaustion, the slipping-back so as to go forward, progress.

The progress in the "Praise to the End" sequence is not
linear, but rather consists of an increased complexity of the
modes of consciousness, an increased capacity to comprehend the world at once in its primeval and in its "civilized"
states. "Where Knock Is Open Wide" ends:

> I'm somebody else now.
> Don't tell my hands.
> Have I come to always? Not yet.
> One father is enough.
>
> Maybe God has a house.
> But not here.

"Bring the Day!," the third poem, ends:

> O small bird wakening,
> Light as a hand among blossoms,
> Hardly any old angels are around any more.
> The air's quiet under the small leaves.
> The dust, the long dust, stays.
> The spiders sail into summer.
> It's time to begin!
> To begin!

"O Lull Me, Lull Me," the sixth and last poem of the sequence, ends:

> Soothe me, great groans of underneath,
> I'm still waiting for a foot.
> The poke of the wind's close,
> But I can't go leaping alone.
> For you, my pond,
> Rocking with small fish,
> I'm an otter with only one nose:
> I'm all ready to whistle;
> I'm more than when I was born;
> I could say hello to things;
> I could talk to a snail;
> I see what sings!
> What sings!

From establishing a sense of place, to a sense of the origin of things, to a sense of proper relationship with things—not separated in natural, organic fact, but only in degree and quality of understanding. The effect is of a man finding and piecing together his knowledge of himself, which is a product of his knowledge of the natural order. Power, then—as we had always known but yet had to discover on our own—is knowledge.

Prefaced by the sequence which I have just discussed, "The Lost Son" serves all the more to celebrate that power. Fleeing from his father, the son turns from a knowledge so violent in its destructiveness as, at the outset, to be beyond comprehension. The poet himself seems to be fleeing from Eliot; for there are here too a number of significant echoes.[4]

---

[4] For example:

> Fished in an old wound,
> The soft pond of repose; . . .

The boy, in any case, flees from "the kingdom of bang and blab" down to a river teeming with primeval creatures; he descends into a pit, where he can "feel the slime of a wet nest"; his world is now one terrifying gibber into whose "dark swirl" he falls. And then, at last, he returns to his father—but now with strength to endure. He can assent to his father's "Ordnung! Ordnung!" to the degree that he understands that the words are necessary, because natural. It is winter; and he lives on, fortified by his memories of what he has learned on his flight—of the spirit within and without himself which he has discovered. In the last poem of the sequence, there is a shift to the second person, where before the first has been used—as though the poet were now sufficiently in possession of himself to achieve a certain objectivity:

> A lively understandable spirit
> Once entertained you.
> It will come again.
> Be still.
> Wait.

At the end, there is a recollection of "Ash-Wednesday." The tranquility in which the recollection comes, however, results from a confrontation, and containment, of the violence within, not—as with Eliot—the violence without.

> Sat in an empty house
> Watching shadows crawl,
> Scratching.
> There was one fly.
> ("The Flight")

and "Where do the roots go? / Look down under the leaves," which, with other such passages, seem to point to *The Waste Land* and "Gerontion"— so that the poem constitutes a kind of reply to Eliot, or an alternative. And Eliot would appear to have remained steadily in Roethke's mind. For "Meditations of an Old Woman" (appearing first as a whole poem in *Words for the Wind*) is surely a reply to *Four Quartets,* which it abundantly echoes.

And the rest of the poems in the "Praise to the End" sequence give analogues of and variations upon this theme. The poem whose title is given to the section celebrates, for the first time in the volume, the power of sexuality. "I'm awake all over:," the poet writes, and continues:

I've crawled from the mire, alert as a saint or a dog;
I know the back-stream's joy, and the stone's eternal pulseless
  longing.
Felicity I cannot hoard. . . .

I believe! I believe!—
In the sparrow, happy on gravel;
In the winter-wasp, pulsing its wings in the sunlight;
I have been somewhere else; I remember the sea-faced uncles.
I hear, clearly, the heart of another singing,
Lighter than bells,
Softer than water.

Wherefore, O birds and small fish, surround me.
Lave me, ultimate waters.
The dark showed me a face.
My ghosts are all gay.
The light becomes me.

These lines mark the poet's sense of his freedom ever after to know, and so to be, himself. Now he is empowered to live in the most possible of all best worlds. Out of the underground dialectic there has emerged a knowledge which is knowing.

Knowing himself in his world, he may know others in theirs and so demonstrate that the two worlds are one. The rest of the poems collected in *Words for the Wind* (about one half the volume) are such demonstrations. They show a degree of formal, "willed" control—a capacity to tighten and loosen movement as syntax will allow it—quite beyond that of the earlier poems. Such poems—even, as regards substance, the most intimate of them—have a certain "public" quality, the assured decorum of the poet as his own kind of noble lord. Consequently, they also have the quality of a certain careless ease. It is the case of the poet as Young Prospero. Only, having read the poems which come before, we know that we are yielding not to the poet's magic but to his wholly earned and deserved authority, an authority which manifests itself as the poet's style. Such authority, indeed, enables him to address himself to subjects nominally banal and commonplace and to rediscover their abiding power for us.

The poems record the visitations of spirits other than the poet's own, his definition of the losses which he must encounter day-to-day, rollicking memories of earlier days, his nursery-rhymed farewell-and-hail to childhood, and, above all, the infinite possibilities of love. Love, indeed, is the essential substance of them all. It is by now, and at long last, the love which can be given and can be received. Love in these poems is different from love in the earlier poems, precisely as its necessary condition is now both giving and receiving. Consciously, willfully to give and to be given to: this initiates the dialectic of relationship to the other which now moves the poems and gives them the formal control which everywhere characterizes them. Their argument is that in love the flesh becomes spirit; that only in time is love possible; that only in love, so known, is eternity to be glimpsed:

> Let seed be grass, and grass turn into hay:
> I'm martyr to a motion not my own;
> What's freedom for? To know eternity.
> I swear she cast a shadow white as stone.

> But who would count eternity in days?
> These old bones live to learn her wanton ways:
> (I measure time by how a body sways).
>   ("I Knew a Woman")

> Dream of a woman, and a dream of death:
> The light air takes my being's breath away;
> I look on white, and it turns into gray—
> When will that creature give me back my breath?
> I live near the abyss. I hope to stay
> Until my eyes look at a brighter sun
> As the thick shade of the long night comes on.
>   ("The Pure Fury")

Just beyond this world, there is a dark world, transcendent, to be discovered. But meantime, there is yet this world, which love makes go round. Roethke, at this stage, was willing to write poem after poem on that truism—in order to bring it back into the life of modern poetry. The pattern and plot that love gives to human life would restore it to its place in the natural order. In "The Waking," he says:

> Great Nature has another thing to do
> To you and me; so take the lively air,
> And, lovely, learn by going where to go.

And in his great sequence, "Four for Sir John Davies," he celebrates (as the Renaissance poet had done before him) the idea of order. For Roethke order is cosmic because sexual, and sexual because cosmic: "The body and the soul know how to play / In that dark world where gods have lost their way." There is then that dark world (elsewhere Roethke calls it an abyss) which threatens, because it awaits. But

> The world is for the living. Who are they?
> We dared the dark to reach the white and warm.
> She was the wind when wind was in my way;
> Alive at noon, I perished in her form.
> Who rise from flesh to spirit know the fall:
> The word outleaps the world, and light is all.
>   ("The Vigil")

This world and the abyss, light and darkness, love and death—the motifs are common enough, as is our sense of their paradoxical coexistence. Roethke's way with the commonplace is to penetrate into its very commonality: to see it in the natural order, to turn inward and backward upon himself and establish his truest involvement in that order, and then to turn outward, to look forward, to fare forward, and, through an understanding of his relation with all that constitutes the other, to affirm that involvement. His reordering of Eliot's formula is this: sympathize, control, give. He would abolish nothing, transmute nothing—but accept everything, and understand as much of it as he can, love even that which he cannot understand. His verse, then, comes to be a vehicle for understanding—and love its principal mode. "Being, not doing, is my first joy," he came to write in a late poem, "The Abyss," even as he felt himself caught up in "The burning heart of the abominable."

In one of the last poems in *Words for the Wind,* a dying man speaks:

> "A man sees, as he dies,
> Death's possibilities;
> My heart sways with the world.
> I am that final thing,
> A man learning to sing."
>   ("His Words")

Roethke's reply is: "A breath is but a breath: I have the
earth; / I shall undo all dying by my death," and

> The edges of the summit still appal
> When we brood on the dead or the beloved;
> Nor can imagination do it all
> In this last place of light: he dares to live
> Who stops being a bird, yet beats his wings
> Against the immense immeasurable emptiness of things.
> ("They Sing, They Sing")

This side of the abyss, the dark world, the edges of the
summit—so far Roethke, in *Words for the Wind,* charted
the journey of his soul. Behind him lay another abyss, into
which he had plunged, another dark world, into which he
had journeyed, another summit, over which he had leaped.
And he had reported fully on his adventures. The reports
are poems; and they are so often major poems because they
are reports become interpretations, characterized by self-
conscious didacticism and a use of traditions and conven-
tions magisterial enough to transfigure, yet not to distort,
the experiences on which they center. It is the poems, not
the poet, which are transfiguring and transfigured. Roethke
seems to have been overwhelmingly aware of the dangers for
the modern poet who would risk the personal heresy. Reading
the poems, one sees him courting that heresy, as it were em-
ploying it against itself. For underpinning the mere person
there is the authentic person. I take Roethke's life-work to
have been directed toward enlarging and deepening the
sense of the authentically personal. On the whole, recent
poets who have been of this persuasion have from the outset
worked to resist threats to their own sacred selves; theirs
has been the violence within fighting the violence without.
Roethke rapidly gave up such a sense of his mission; and

taught himself (somehow) that first he must learn not to resist himself. Everything followed.

It did not follow as far as it should have. It did not follow
as his work promises it would. Our tragedy is that, dying,
Roethke did not come to write the poems which would have
undone death—I mean the component of death as in his
poems he came more and more to acknowledge its immiti-
gable existence. His poems controlled, they sympathized.
They only began, at the end, fully to give. They controlled
the wide and deep areas of the personal, the widest and deepest, I am persuaded, in the work of any contemporary
American poet. And they demonstrated again and again how
we have access to those areas only through sympathy—the
power of human sympathy as it at first derives and then
differentiates itself from the power which maintains the natural order of things. Roethke began to learn, and to make
poems which teach, that out of the power of sympathy there
comes the power to give, thus to be given to. He began to
comprehend the full range of the other, that chain of being
which moves from the minimal to God.

The poems in *The Far Field* indicate the distance he had
come. Many of the love poems are centered on the consciousness of woman, an "I" different enough from the center of consciousness of the earlier love poems to manifest
not only the power of sympathy but of identity with another. In the process, the poet's separate identity is not lost
but, for the sake of the poems and the world they create,
put aside. The feminine speaker in these poems has little to
do with the exacerbated speculations of the masculine
speaker of the earlier ones. As the poet gives her to us, we
sense that she has always been steadily enough in touch with
her interior past (the past of "Where Knock Is Open Wide"
and the rest) to have let herself live, and give, fully in the
presence of others:

> We are one, and yet we are more,
> I am told by those who know,—
> At times content to be two.
>> ("The Young Girl")

> Before this longing,
> I lived serene as a fish,
> At one with the plants in the pond,
> The mare's tail, the floating frogbit,
> Among my eight-legged friends,
> Open like a pool, a lesser parsnip,
> Like a leech, looping myself along,
> A bug-eyed edible one,
> A mouth like a stickleback,—
> A thing quiescent!

> But now—
> The wild stream, the sea itself cannot contain me. . . .
>> ("Her Longing")

And the poet, as the masculine speaker in some of the poems, has learned too, because he has discovered his beloved as she is necessarily part of the order of great nature:

> My lizard, my lively writher,
> May your limbs never wither,
> May the eyes in your face
> Survive the green ice
> Of envy's mean gaze;
> May you live out your life
> Without hate, without grief,
> And your hair ever blaze,
> In the sun, in the sun,
> When I am undone,
> When I am no one.
>> ("Wish for a Young Wife")

He learns that he must some day be no one. And he knows his own temporal oneness all the more specifically, as he knows that of those who people his world—Aunt Tilly whom he celebrates in an "Elegy"; the heroic "Otto" and all those who have inhabited "my father's world,— / O world so far away! O my lost world!"; and, simply enough, his "Chums":

> Some are in prison; some are dead;
>   And none has read my books,
> And yet my thoughts turn back to them. . . .

What matters is that such memories no longer threaten. Again, he can write of the dark world, but now with the control which comes from loving understanding. Indeed, now he is ready to establish the crucial identification for the American poet:

> Be with me, Whitman, maker of catalogues:
> For the world invades me again,
> And once more the tongues begin babbling.
> And the terrible hunger for objects quails me. . . .

This passage is from a poem I have already cited, "The Abyss." The manner, the structure, and the movement are superficially like such terrified poems as "Where Knock Is Open Wide." But there is now available to the poet a capacity for objectification, itself a product of a capacity for meditation—meditation outward, as it were. "Too much reality can be a dazzle, a surfeit," he writes, and follows this with: "Too close immediacy an exhaustion." He is free, however, to move through the abyss of exhaustion to the peace beyond, which is the peace of acceptance:

> I thirst by day. I watch by night.
> I receive! I have been received!
> I hear the flowers drinking in their light,
> I have taken counsel of the crab and the sea-urchin. . . .

Again the order of nature—now most surely an ordering, so that the conclusion must come:

> I am most immoderately married:
> The Lord God has taken my heaviness away;
> I have merged, like the bird, with the bright air,
> And my thought flies to the place by the bo-tree.

> Being, not doing, is my first joy.

There are two grand efforts toward synthesis in *The Far Field*. Perfected achievements in themselves, the two poems are nonetheless prolegomena toward poems which Roethke did not live to write, toward a synoptic vision of the condition of modern man which at the end was yet beyond him. In the "North American Sequence," the poet is first the explorer of the natural order; then a part of it; then an explorer into the interior of his own experience, so conceived; then the poet who can "embrace the world"; then the poet who realizes that "He is the end of things, the final man"; [5] then he who has been given—or, in his struggle, has given

[5] The whole passage would seem at once to echo and to salute the later Wallace Stevens, whom Roethke claimed (in his uncollected "Rouse" for Stevens) as a father-figure for poets of his generation:

> The lost self changes,
> Turning toward the sea,
> A sea-shape turning around,—
> An old man with his feet before the fire,
> In robes of green, in garments of adieu.

> A man faced with his own immensity
> Wakes all the waves, all their loose wandering fire.
> The murmur of the absolute, the why
> Of being born fails on his naked ears.
> His spirit moves like monumental wind
> That gentles on a sunny blue plateau.
> He is the end of things, the final man.
> ("The Far Field")

This is Roethke's version of the "hero," "the final man," celebration of whom dominates much of Stevens' later verse.

himself—unmediated vision into the very center of being. The argument of the "North American Sequence" works to unify, and to make all of a piece, the world which has invaded the poet, so as to allow him to invade it. The experience would not seem to be ecstatic; for nothing has been cast off. On the contrary, everything has been grasped at once and together, gloriously; and such unification has become the very process of summing-up. The poet (his mentor is still Whitman) discovers that he is part of that sum, that sacred sum. Thus, at the end:

Near this rose, in this grove of sun-parched, wind-warped madronas,
Among the half-dead trees, I came upon the true ease of myself,
As if another man appeared out of the depths of my being,
And I stood outside myself,
Beyond becoming and perishing,
A something wholly other,
As if I swayed out on the wildest wave alive,
And yet was still.
And I rejoiced in being what I was:
In the lilac change, the white reptilian calm,
In the bird beyond the bough, the single one
With all the air to greet him as he flies,
The dolphin rising from the darkening waves;

And in this rose, this rose in the sea-wind,
Rooted in stone, keeping the whole of light,
Gathering to itself sound and silence—
Mine and the sea-wind's.

("The Rose")

The compulsion here, as so often in Roethke's later work, is toward the sacred. The underground dialectic, at once empowered and constrained by the poet's dedication to the ordering of nature, has evolved an idea of God. The "Sequence,

Sometimes Metaphysical" treats of that idea. In "In a Dark
Time" (as in the last poem in the "North American Sequence") the poet encounters himself as one object among
many. They constitute "A steady storm of correspondences,"
and in their storming put to the deepest doubt his sense of the
order of nature—as though the order of nature, if only one
knows it unmediated, as it really is, might negate itself, and
issue into the ultimate entropy. His doubt now is like that
which came to him when he confronted for the first time the
possibility of his own authentic existence and that of the
persons, places, and things which constituted his world:

> Dark, dark my light, and darker my desire.
> My soul, like some heat-maddened summer fly,
> Keeps buzzing at the sill. Which I is *I?*
> A fallen man, I climb out of my fear.
> The mind enters itself, and God the mind,
> And one is One free in the tearing wind.

The logic here is keen. Encountering himself as object, man
fights through his terror and so rises from his fallen state.
He knows once and for all that the price he has to pay for
discovering God as object is the same as that he has had to
pay for encountering as object any of the forms of the
other: the old divisive agony of meditation. Yet now he has
the strength, the power, to will himself into understanding
and to make whole what has been divided—himself. So
doing, he brings God into his "mind." But now he knows that
it is he who has found God, he who has redeemed Him, and
made manifest His freedom in that "tearing wind."

Such, I take it, is the central motif in the "Sequence,
Sometimes Metaphysical." The "Godhead above my God"
whom the poet addresses in "The Marrow" is the source of
the power which the poet has always sought; finding it, he
will have found the means to redeem the God below:

> I was flung back from suffering and love
> When light divided on a storm-tossed tree;
> Yea, I have slain my will, and still I live;
> I would be near; I shut my eyes to see;
> I bleed my bones, their marrow to bestow
> Upon the God who knows what I would know.

The other poems in the sequence are less "metaphysical" than these two, perhaps; but they nonetheless celebrate those moments of meditation, with its burden of divisiveness, which are the necessary consequences of the poet's search for, and likewise the necessary antecedents of, his discovery of the sacred. For always he demands—"More! O More! visible." He goes on in this poem:

> Now I adore my life
> With the Bird, the abiding Leaf,
> With the Fish, the questing Snail,
> And the Eye altering all;
> And I dance with William Blake
> For love, for Love's sake;
>
> And everything comes to One,
> As we dance on, dance on, dance on.
>   ("Once More, the Round")

I have said that the poems in *The Far Field* indicate how far Roethke had come. They may also indicate how far he might have gone. In the note of explanation he wrote for John Ciardi's anthology, *Mid-Century American Poets* (1950), Roethke concluded: "The next phase? Something much longer: dramatic and *playable*. Pray for me." He did not live long enough to reach that phase. In his last poems, he did discover one of the necessary means to the dramatic: a full sense of the other. But the discovery was longer in the making, and surely more painful, than he seems to have imagined it would be. For whatever reason, he could not undertake the compulsive twentieth-century quest for identity via the route of alienation—which, we are told, is in our time the only proper route for the man of high imagination. His was the way of sympathy, and he kept to it as long as he lived. In his work, there are many moments of alienation; but they are associated with violence, and he works to transform the violence into power, thus alienation into identification.

Had he lived longer, he might have written a poem of power and identification, a *Jerusalem* for our age. Truly, his beginning was in his end. Even his discovery of God, the ultimate other, could promise him no respite. For God had to be fought toward, and the fighting-toward threatened always to be a fighting against: if not against God, against man. But Roethke was always bound not to be against. . . . The ordering of the "Sequence, Sometimes Metaphysical" registers just this movement, and proves it out. Thus I suggest that perhaps Roethke would have turned to Blake as his great model. (He was always nobly blatant in his study of models.) Calling to mind Blake's *Tiriel*, he pleads with Mnetha (whom Foster Damon calls Blake's Athena), mother of Har (whom Damon calls poetry degenerated), in "The Long Waters" section of the "North American Sequence." And he associates himself with Blake in "Once More, the Round," the last poem in the "Sequence, Sometimes Metaphysical." Perhaps, then, his vision would have become as large as Blake's; and, like Blake, he would have been able to put into his poems the awareness of the concrete and particular conditions of modern life, the biting hatred of abusers of power, even the wonderful comedy which, as he selected his poems for *Words for the Wind,* for the most part he

set aside. A Blakean poem—narrative, prophetic, lyric, di-
atribic—we may guess, was his life's project, as was his
life. For him the world was first I, then (from the minimal to
God) thou—but not yet, as with Blake, he, she, or they.
Learning the lessons of his work, we can say only that in
our time, the world (too much with us) is inhabited by third
persons, fearing to be first, therefore unable to reach toward
the second.

To have revealed the sacredness of the second person, of
all persons (and places and things) as they in truth are second—this is Roethke's achievement. And more than that: to
have made known that our world of third persons is one in
which the power of sympathy, if it exists outside the order
of nature, becomes one of violence, now murderous, now sui-
cidal, now both; to have transformed suicide into a means
of rebirth and rediscovery; to have "undone" death, and to
have dared to "do" love. Freed in the process, Roethke
might have indeed become his own kind of Blake.

In a posthumously published piece (*Encounter*, Decem-
ber, 1963)—it was intended to be one of the "Winterset
Rothberg" tirades—Roethke, in fact, wrote in the mode of
Blake's *Descriptive Catalogues*. He addressed his "more
tedious contemporaries":

> Roaring asses, hysterics, sweet-myself beatniks, earless wonders happy
> with effects a child of two could improve on: verbal delinquents; snig-
> gering, mildly obscene souser-wowsers, this one writing as if only he
> had a penis, that one bleeding, but always in waltz-time; another in-
> toning, over and over, in metres the expert have made hideous; the
> doleful, almost-good, over-trained technicians—what a mincing ex-
> plicitness, what a profusion of adjectives, what a creaking of adverbs!

He went on in this vein, and at length, telling the violent
truth. Yet at the end, in Blake's manner, he shifted to verse,
characterized by his immense power of sympathy.

Was it reading you I first felt, full in my face, the hot blast and
    clatter of insane machinery?
Yet heard,
Beneath the obscene murderous noise of matter gone mad,
Whose grinding dissonance threatens to overwhelm us all,
The small cry of the human?

I, the loneliest semi-wretch alive, a stricken minor soul,
Weep to you now;
But I've an eye to your leaping forth and fresh ways of wonder;
And I see myself beating back and forth like stale water in a
    battered pail;
Are not you my final friends, the fair cousins I loathe and love?
That man hammering I adore, though his noise reach the very walls
    of my inner self;
Behold, I'm a heart set free, for I have taken my hatred and eaten it,
The last acrid sac of my rat-like fury;
I have succumbed, like all fanatics, to my imagined victims;
I embrace what I perceive!
Brothers and sisters, dance ye,
Dance ye all!

To have heard always the small cry of the human and to
have amplified it and extended its range—that, as things
came to stand with Roethke, had to be enough.